Beautiful Body, Beautiful *Mind*

The Power of Positive Imagery

With over 80 exercises and a
10-day beauty program

Beautiful Body, Beautiful Mind

The Power of Positive Imagery

With over 80 exercises and a
10-day beauty program

Eric Franklin

Illustrated by Sonja Burger
and Eric Franklin

Translated by Lorna Dunn and Gisela Weismann

Elysian Editions
Princeton Book Company, Publishers

Please note:
This book will help you become more flexible. It provides information that can help you to help yourself. It does not replace medical advice. When in doubt, experiencing sustained or acute pain, or suffering from illness, you should consult a doctor or other qualified health professional.

Originally published as *Denk dich jung!*
© 2005 für die deutsche Ausgabe by VAK Verlags GmbH, Kirchzarten

Elysian Editions
Princeton Book Company, Publishers
614 Route 130
Hightstown, NJ 08520

Translated by Lorna Dunn and Gisela Weismann
Illustrated by Sonja Burger and Eric Franklin

Interior Design and Composition by Mulberry Tree Press
Cover design by Maria M. Mann, High Tide Design

Publisher's Cataloging-In-Publication Data
(Prepared by The Donohue Group, Inc.)

Franklin, Eric N.
   [Denk dich jung! English]
   Beautiful body, beautiful mind : the power of positive imagery : with over 80 exercises and a 10-day beauty program / Eric Franklin ; illustrated by Sonja Burger and Eric Franklin ; translated by Lorna Dunn and Gisela Weismann.

      p. : ill. ; cm.

   Translation of: Denk dich jung! Kirchzarten :VAK-Verlags, 2005.
   Includes index of exercises.
   ISBN: 978-0-87127-309-3

1. Mind and body. 2. Imagery (Psychology) 3. Relaxation. 4. Motivation (Psychology) I. Burger, Sonja. II. Dunn, Lorna. III. Weismann, Gisela. IV. Title. V. Title: Denk dich jung!

BF367 .F7313 2009
153.32

Printed in the United States of America.

8 7 6 5 4 3 2 1

Contents

Introduction: Finding Eternal Youth with Movement and Imagination

The Allure of Eternal Youth

Anti-aging and rejuvenation appeal today as never before. From face lifting to mud treatments, from cell therapy to juice diets, the aim of each is to reverse the clock. While this is not a bad goal, it is at times short-sighted. Beauty magazines and other publications are packed with advertisements for cosmetics and cosmetic surgery. New dietary supplements appear regularly as well as old supplements in new packages.

I have nothing against these methods. However, acquiring pricey cosmetics, choosing the best surgeon, or tracking down the most potent vitamins all require time and money. In some cases, there is also documented risk. A surgical procedure might not produce the desired result; a vitamin supplement can be overdosed or ineffective. For a long and healthy life, the single most important factor appears to be lifestyle: the physical habits and mental attitudes of everyday life.

With this in mind, the Franklin Method® is presented here with no further investment than this book and your own imaginative powers. You will experience what you can do to stay youthful without scalpels, creams, and pills. The emphasis is on *lifestyle* and *mental attitude*. Central to the Franklin Method® are *movement* and use of the *imagination*. **Imagery is what allows us to picture movement, both that which has taken place and that which may take place in the future.** With the help of the imagination, we make sense of the world around us, plan and weigh the advisability, or lack thereof, of our next actions. That which we regularly present to our inward eye and convincingly train ourselves to see may be actually realized in our daily lives. **This is the basis of imaginative suggestion.** The athlete pictures herself or himself on the podium with a gold medal, the ill envisage a speedy recovery, the dancer multiple pirouettes. And Seiryu Noguchi (1900–2005), still physically and mentally active at age 105, spoke about going to bed each night imagining with anticipation the next day's activities in the garden: "My head is filled with all the things I want to do tomorrow."

Genetics, Behavior and Imagination

During the last thirty years, the imagination has been the subject of considerable scientific interest and recognition. Thousands of studies have vouched for its potent effects. New publications regularly appear, revealing its powerful influence on our physical and emotional health, and by extension, our accomplishments. One of the world's largest research organizations, the United States National Institutes of Health (or NIH) regularly promotes its findings in *mind-body medicine,* as this growing branch of medicine is known. The National Cancer Institute, an office of the NIH, supports the use of imagery as a method helpful in fighting the effects of cancer. The Franklin Method® Institute has conducted imagery classes for dancers at such venues as the Juilliard School in New York, the Royal Ballet in London, England, and the School of the Royal Danish Ballet in Copenhagen, Denmark. A wide spectrum of participants, young and not so young, amateur and professional, benefit from our training in the applied use of imagery at our Institute in Switzerland and classes worldwide.

Our imagination is especially effective in maintaining a youthful physique, because it can expose, relieve, and even prevent chronic problems. Those who enjoy the accumulated effects of lifelong investment in physical and emotional health have reached a special level indeed. Keeping the body and soul in good running order allows one to live longer and with more enjoyment. The goal is to extend the shelf life of your body by making sure that the mental and physical impacts on your body are indeed the most healthful. Boston University's Thomas Perls (quoted from a 2001 CNN interview), geriatrician and one of the founding directors of the *New England Centenarian Study,* has said that his work disproves the common belief that "the older you get the sicker you get." Rather, "the older you get, the healthier you've been." So the more healthily one lives, the longer and better one lives. Genetic factors count for no more than twenty to thirty percent in aging, established through studies of identical twins. Despite great physical similarities, the life span of twins can differ individually according to style of living.

The bottom line: a healthy life is more than anything related to behavior, mirrored in the quality of our thoughts and daily activities. When these factors are combined with healthful nutrition, the chances for a long life are very good. This book offers an abundance of information to improve the quality of our physical and mental habits. (I will touch on the subject of nutrition only briefly as there is a wealth of material already available on the subject.)

Chapter 1: The Power of Suggestion

To begin, we will look more closely at how to mobilize the power of our thoughts and imagination. Then we will go for a stroll through the body to experience how such application can help to keep our joints, muscles, organs, glands, and nerves in life-long healthful working order.

Mobilizing Imaginative Power

There are different ways to think about the applied use of imagery. For some it denotes mental discipline as a means to life enhancement, for others a way to maximize physical output; still others see it as a relaxation technique.

"Imagery" needs first to be clarified. The training applied to our *Beautiful Body/Beautiful Mind* program is scientifically researched and includes mental simulation of movement, anatomical and metaphorical imagery, self-talk, goal-setting, motivational techniques, and relaxation. You will be introduced to intuitive imagery and to the use of imagery to improve flexibility, posture, and health of the joints, muscles and organs.

With the assistance of embodied imagery, we can tone muscles, influence digestion, activate hormones, adjust and modulate cerebral activity, and much more.

The extensive network of diverse techniques allows the Franklin Method® a very high success rate. The speed of success depends on your ability to create vivid imagery, but luckily fundamental imagery skills are inborn and can be applied immediately. For most beginners it takes about ten days to see clearly successful results. However, I have known many instances where within minutes flexibility will increase and pain disappears, or where a participant will suddenly feel refreshed. Once the practice becomes familiar, imagination works quickly: one *thinks it* and the result is already in place.

We will begin now with some practical application. I have arranged the first exercises into an overview of the imagination (as it is applied to the Franklin Method®). In this way, you can experience it immediately.

Concentration

Concentration is the starting point for every technique that uses imagery. If we are not aware or *present*, neither can we consciously imagine. Being present allows us to be cognizant of immediate processes taking place in the body and mind, and by using the imagination, to alter them. For many people with chronic pain, the applied use of concentration (especially in breathing) enables successful pain management.

A breath at the tip of the nose

Choose a specific part of your body such as the right knee, the heel of the left foot, or as in the following example, the tip of the nose. Concentrate entirely on the air flowing in and out of the tip of the nose. Remain focused for one minute on this stream of air. Think only of this airy passage. Afterward, you will find your breathing more restful. Perhaps you were not entirely successful and followed stray thoughts as they floated through your mind. Practice the exercise again, choosing another point of concentration. With time, your concentration will become deeper and longer lasting, and you will reach your objectives sooner.

Activating the Senses

A chef sniffs and savors a soup before serving it; a musician hears a melody in his or her mind before playing it. In our imagination, we picture our dream house or partner. This sweetheart massages our shoulders (mmm... better already!) We sit in a Jacuzzi, listen to birds sing, and catch the aroma of nearby flowers; we consider getting out but for the time being decide against it.

With all of the above, we used the sense organs to imagine:

Smell (olfactory);

Taste (gustatory);

Sounds (auditory);

Seeing an image (visual);

The feel of a massage (tactile);

Positional sense while sitting in a Jacuzzi (proprioceptive);

Motion: climbing out of a Jacuzzi (kinesthetic);

The chill of a breeze while standing by a Jacuzzi (thermal).

While some of these images were *inside* the body—the imagined music and the relaxing massage for example—others, like the bubbling water, were *outside* the body. Still others can penetrate the body's surface from outside, as when you imagine warm and relaxing sunrays penetrating deep inside you. Certain images can become larger or smaller. A lovely butterfly flies toward you (becoming larger); something is written in colored letters on its wings, this gets larger and larger and will soon be clearly visible. To behold in the imagination these patterned fluttering wings, you have created a precise image called a *local image*. If the butterfly takes off and flies away it becomes smaller and smaller. Eventually all you see is the sky which fills your whole visual image. This large expanse is a *global image*. Another example of a kinesthetic global image is imagining yourself floating in the water at a beautiful beach. Since you feel the water all around you the image is global. If you imagine one of your feet touching the sandy underground, the image is local—in one specific place only.

Hearing compliments in our imagination

Test for yourself how auditive imagery can improve your mood. One morning, before beginning the day, hear in your imagination how others respond to your appearance: "Oh, you look terrific today! I can see that things are going well for you. You really look good. Have you been on a vacation? You look so rested. I think you must be in love!" and so on.

Use expressions such as these, or experiment with others that might suit you better. See and hear the people who speak these words. The speakers can be fictitious or be someone you know. Perhaps at first you will find it absurd or corny to imagine such things. The effect, though, is surprisingly beneficial. People will actually start responding differently to you than before. They will notice your inner disposition, even if they cannot quite put their finger on its source. A worthwhile experiment.

The effects of sugar pills — just vanity?

Imaginary compliments are most effective when you have a specific task in mind, for example a lecture or speech. Athletic or artistic endeavors also benefit from this or from similar preparation beforehand. This has nothing to do with the superficiality of conceit, but with positive expectations. That our expectations have considerable influence on the body has been shown in numerous placebo studies. In such studies a medicine is usually tested against a substance with no curative powers of its own, often a sugar pill. In a particularly astonishing experiment of this type, patients in an emergency room were informed that their prescribed medicine was in reality a sugar pill. Although told that the pill was only sugar, evidence showed that many patients improved regardless. In all patients the symptoms abated, thanks to the sugar pill 'medicine', save one whose husband had convinced her *not* to take the pill because it was nothing but humbug.

Effective Imagery for All the Senses

The better endowed our imagination in its ability to stimulate or relate to the senses, the more effective it is. An example of a relatively ineffective image is the following: "Imagine you are a rock." The sense of movement and the senses that affect change in your body´s disposition are not sufficiently addressed.

Imagining yourself to have a slim and trim waistline and a six-pack abdomen makes more sense for most people as it carries meaning and elicits a positive emotional response. Surprisingly a trim waistline, or more specifically the lack of belly fat, has been associated with better brain function as one ages (in "Forgetting is the New Normal", *Time* Magazine, June 30, 2008).

An example of an olfactory/tactile/gustatory image that will elicit a sensory response is "You are now biting into an apple." You sense the pulp on your gums, the tartness on your tongue and between your teeth, the zesty aroma. (Is your mouth watering reading this?)

A functional image produces a physically perceptible response. This is especially the case when imagined situations or images have a relevant meaning or an emotional context.

Biological and metaphorical imagery

In the Franklin Method® we distinguish between *biological* and *metaphorical* (Greek, to transfer) imagery. This distinction is sometimes called direct and indirect. In the first instance, imagination relates directly to the anatomical (real) body; in the second, the body is metaphorically transformed in order to create a more comprehensive experience of the image. Biological imagery can be further subdivided into anatomical, biomechanical and chemical imagery. Biomechanical imagery describes the movement of the joints and muscles; chemical imagery relates to the metabolic activities of the body.

Metaphorical imagery is often very helpful to those unfamiliar with human anatomy. One reason that this imagery can so favorably influence health is that illness, for whatever reason, may be perceived on a symbolic level as pictures that carry a particular meaning. If one alters the symbolism and imagery that affect our health, organic function is likewise transformed. Our societal and cultural environment influences the symbols we ascribe to illness.

If you imagine your lungs expanding and contracting with each breath you are using a biological, or to be more precise, anatomical image. If you are imagining the lungs to be sponges that are expanding and contracting, the image is metaphorical, and since it is still very close to the real function it is anatomically equivalent or related. If you imagine a joint between your lungs and heart (the lung being the socket and the heart the ball), then you are imagining biomechanically. If, however, you imagine your breath traveling up and down your body as colorful waves of light, you are using a metaphor that is not related to anatomy.

Unfortunately for many people, certain areas of the body carry negative associations. The spine and back are a classic example. Many people associate the back with images of pain, stiffness, cramping, herniation, scoliosis and sciatica—in short, with negative images and words and the symbolism that goes with them. Seldom do I hear such a positive exclamation as: "Today my back feels supple and resilient, lengthened, flexible and strong. It is lovely to experience my intervertebral discs as cushiony, balanced and supportive." Images like this can be genuinely attained only after some practice—as distant as we are from positive expectations concerning our back. The first step in healing your back or creating lifelong health for your back is to create a positive plan for your spine and back. (Please see below).

With practice, you will see that biological and metaphorical imagery are invaluable tools for a healthier body. The ability to picture organic structures and functions can achieve amazing results in terms of healing and rejuvenation. An example of this can be seen in a study of asthma patients. The best results in managing the condition were achieved by participants who created images of supportive cellular activity.

The imagery chosen by those asthma patients was chemical. They imagined their cells remaining calm and unaffected by attack-stimulating agents (histamines).

To understand the difference between biological and metaphorical imagery, we will practice releasing the shoulders.

Releasing the shoulders

Place your right hand on the left shoulder (arm in front), near your neck where the muscles are more thickly layered, rather than on the shoulder joint itself. Make small circles with the left shoulder, keeping in mind that the shoulder is seventy percent water. Water is, of course, fluid, so make the circles as if watching water ebb and flow in response to the movement. This is an example of anatomical imagery, that is, imagery that parallels actual circumstance. Now circle the shoulder in the other direction, noticing that your breathing is becoming progressively more peaceful.

With the right hand in the same place on the relaxed shoulder, gently squeeze the muscles with the fingers as if squeezing a sponge. Imagine all tension in the shoulder being squeezed out through this sponge. Now release the fingers and then the entire hand. Slowly let go of the 'sponge' and imagine water flowing back as it is reabsorbed, while the 'muscle sponge' fills out and spreads and widens.

We have just made use of metaphorical imagery, with the sponge as a metaphor for muscular relaxation. Repeat the exercise 3 more times. Squeeze the sponge with the right hand to empty it. Release the hand, allowing the muscles to fill once more with water (as would a sponge) and to open out fully. After the third repetition, remove the hand, shake it out, and notice if there is a difference between the two shoulders.

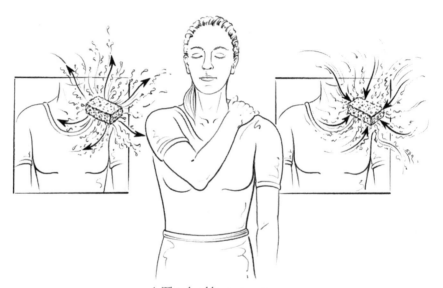

1. The shoulder as sponge

The shoulder-as-sponge exercise described above has led to one shoulder feeling more relaxed than the other. This is the result of the exercise itself; the outcome could not have been foreseen with accuracy beforehand. If the sensation is pleasant, relaxation can be absorbed all the sooner into our new body image with upright posture and relaxed shoulders. It is important to take in your new state with awareness, as this allows your brain to absorb the sensations and record them as your new state of being.

How long will the effects of an exercise last? It depends upon how successful we are at integrating sensation into our body image. Integration will be accomplished if we really like the new sensation, live daily with it, and move beyond classifying it as a momentary experience. How I behave is who I am. Aging depends largely on behavior. If a stooped back and rigid shoulders are normal for you, or part of your identity, the benefit of any exercise will be temporary. The goal is to maintain your new body image and accept it as the new you. At the same time, make sure to fend off old habits that may attempt to reestablish themselves.

Returning to the example above, repeat the shoulder-as-sponge exercise whenever you feel your shoulders locking up. Do it until a released condition is normal for you. Letting go of physical tension correlates to successful aging: letting go of anger at life, with all its irksome trials. Anger produces chemicals in the body that cause us to age more quickly. And who with upright posture and relaxed, soft shoulders can really be enraged?

Creating change in your body: the four steps

Creating change in your body with the Franklin Method® proceeds with four steps. First you notice your state of being, the status quo of your body. You become aware of what you like about your body and what your challenges are. Then you plan how you would actually like to feel, look and move. Write the plan for your body in a journal and create precise and vivid descriptions. Then you implement your plan through your thoughts, images and movement. Finally you notice the results and, if you like them, integrate them into your body image. If you do not, adjust your plans to create better results.

These can also be called:

1. the feedback stage (noticing your state of being);
2. the creative stage (planning);
3. the feed-forward stage (feeding your plan into your actions) and
4. the comparison stage (do you like the results, and if not, adjust your feed-forward).

Feedback and feed-forward

Without feedback, the act of noticing your state of being, you cannot realize or discover what needs to change. Often what needs to be changed is obvious: you have pain, a movement restriction, bad posture, and so forth. Sometimes you need to practice self-observation to start noticing where a problem is coming from.

Feedback comes in three fundamental forms: the thoughts in your head, the images and feelings you have about your body, and your emotional state. As an example of feedback you may be thinking: my shoulders are collapsed and my belly sticks out. You see and feel yourself with that posture, and you may feel bad about yourself on an emotional level. Now if you feel that this is the way you are and that it cannot be changed you are already feeding these three states forward into the future, in other words, perpetuating it. To break this cycle you need to change your feed-forward by imagining the following: my shoulders are lifting and balancing, my belly is now becoming flat. Then you picture yourself in this state, feel yourself in your body in this new state, and notice your new and happier emotional state.

Posture and the look and feeling of youthfulness have a lot to do with each other. Most people have an image of the elderly as stooped and shrunken. However, many young people have an equally slouched posture. No matter how old you are, bad posture is bad for your health and can be improved by using biomechanical imagery. Good posture is also elegant and attractive; bad posture on the other hand may even arouse anxiety in certain people.

Endorphins and well-being

To describe chemical imagery, we must first discuss the power of endorphins. Endorphins are the body's own natural drug used to combat stress and pain. Chemically they are classified as *polypeptides* (protein chains of amino acids). When endorphins are circulating in the body, we feel terrific. The 'high' of the endurance athlete, running for hours with no apparent effort, is courtesy of endorphins. In sexual activity, endorphins produce feelings of euphoria and during childbirth they reduce the pain of labor. Endorphins can also be released in response to touch, laughter, concentration (meditation), breathing exercises, and suggestive imagery. Studies have shown that endorphins can be released with the help of imagery and expectation. Endorphins are the reason placebos (substances with no curative power of their own) can alleviate pain. Belief and expectation stimulate the brain to produce these natural painkillers. (Source: www.wissenschaft.de, 24.8.2005)

The cerebral aqueduct and the pituitary

Endorphins are hormones, and they are produced in the body in several places. Two of these sites are the pituitary gland, also known as the *hypophysis*, and in nerve cells (called periaqueductal grey matter) surrounding an area called the cerebral aqueduct. The pituitary, which looks like a little grape hanging from a stem beneath the hypothalamus, has multiple functions and produces fourteen or more hormonally active substances. The cerebral aqueduct is a canal-like structure in the brain stem that links the third and fourth cerebral ventricles. Ventricles are cavities deep in the brain that produce and circulate cerebral spinal fluid. This specialized fluid protects and nourishes the brain and spinal cord.

Imagining endorphin activity

Now for an example of chemical imagery: imagine a large droplet of endorphin budding like dew on the pituitary. Think of laughing uproariously; you are shaking with laughter. Remember the last time you laughed like this! Your laughter causes the droplet to fall and endorphins to disperse throughout the body. They stream from the pituitary to distribute feelings of wellness and delight.

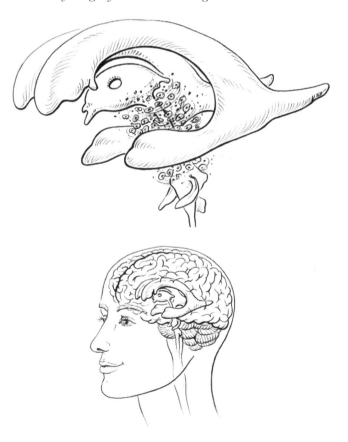

2. The cerebral aqueduct and surrounding structures

Now imagine the ventricles, cavities filled with cerebral spinal fluid. Take a stroll with your inner eye through this cavernous place, observing the walls and the wondrous cells of the brain. On the surface of certain cells, a great bustle of activity is taking place: messages of well being are packaged there for send-off.

Picture these cells throwing off endorphins like ocean spray. The endorphins disperse and their messages flow to wherever they are needed. Feelings of pain and anxiety are replaced by wellness and even euphoria. As each stress vanishes, what remains is breath and refreshing, healthful tranquility.

Motivation and Rejuvenation

Motivation is a key factor in athletics, in everyday life and health in general. Those who are motivated achieve their objectives more easily and enjoy life more fully. When are we motivated and when not? This is an important question and will be the subject of some lively scientific debate and analysis. In sport, motivation can be used to reach different goals. These might include attaining a specific goal, improving self-confidence, or the goal of successfully preparing oneself for a task. Such aims are important in everyday life as well. Motivated people are happier and happy people more motivated. Motivation encourages stronger immune systems: responding to immunization, they evidently produce more antibodies. They are more hopeful and optimistic, and these mental attitudes in turn influence attitudes to health.

Studies in longevity have likewise shown that individuals who reach an advanced age are almost invariably motivated and active in the world around them. In one such study, those who considered their age to be a positive factor, lived on average 7.5 years longer. A further study in Holland showed that there was a reduced risk of death for those with a positive outlook by an average of 50 percent! With regard to posture, joints, organs and muscles, motivation improves health.

So I hope that you are now motivated: motivated to live healthfully. The only question is whether increased motivation can spring, just like that, from your current state of being. The answer for most of us is a definite "Yes." We will begin with some clear objectives.

Motivation and goals

It is an interesting discovery that in terms of the body, most people do not have clearly imagined goals. When teaching, I often ask the course participants, "When you go on vacation, do you make plans in advance? Do you know where and when you will go and how you will get there?" Most have a picture of what to expect, or at least what to hope for and antici-pate. But if, in the same breath, I ask about goals and expectations in regard to the back, not much is forthcoming besides possibly, "No pain". The neg-ative aspect alone of this statement would hinder us from reaching any ob-jective. I then give an example of a clear and positive objective: "My goal is that my back will be flexible, balanced and strong and feel fabulous in all my activities. Within six months I want to experience my back strong and mobile." This sort of declaration usually produces nervous laughter. Why is this? Because the idea is so foreign. When, in the normal course of life, does one hear such fulsome positive notions regarding the back? Most people only refer to it when there is a problem. We should therefore not be sur-prised if our backs are not doing too well. Our well-researched methods come to the rescue with positive goals.

The more varied, precise, and vivid the means to your objective, (with imagery for all the senses), the sooner it will be realized. If you make a New Year's resolution of health, and include in it a fully detailed picture of what this word means for you, you will have begun a program of much potential benefit.

Take five minutes right now (it will be worthwhile), to write a clear profile of how you see your health in six months:

How will you feel?
What will you be thinking about?
How will you look?
How will your joints and muscles feel?
How are your inner organs doing?
How strong and flexible are you?
How will those around you respond to your appearance?

If you find it difficult to come up with words and objectives, read this book from cover to cover. Along the way, you can pick up and select a colorful array of images and aspirations for every part of the body.

Preparing your goals

Goals are most attainable when set in the not-too-distant future. Certainly it does no harm to say, "In ten years my back will be in great shape." To suf-fer back pain for nine years of that time before finally doing something

3. Left: poorly imagined goals; Right: well imagined goals

about it would be, however, most certainly a shame. Set your sights on reaching a goal within several weeks, months, or at most, a year.

Plan goals realistically. If you have sciatica and tell yourself, "In fifteen minutes I will be in peak condition, my body in perfect shape from head to toe," it is not really convincing. Anything is possible, of course, but it might be more helpful to say, "By the end of the week I will be well again. I will move with ease and flexibility."

Goals should not be based on comparison with other people: "I would like my back to be stronger and more flexible than X's." Again, generalized aspirations such as "I should be doing better" are never as effective as clearly defined goals that are multi-faceted and colored with imagination.

Motivation, self-confidence and posture

To understand the link between posture and mood, try this short experiment:

Slouch down and say aloud, "I'm doing well and I feel wonderful." You can feel that your posture and the assertion do not match.

Now raise your arms overhead, hands and fingers stretched long, your spine also straight and pulled up. In this posture say, "I feel tired and miserable." Here too you can feel the difference between posture and assertion. A person who is cheerful and self-confident stands up straighter.

Motivation, self-confidence and flexibility

Our disposition has an immediate effect on flexibility and resilience. This can mean lightning-quick steps to rejuvenation. That youth and resilience go together needs no explanation. I propose that with directed thought we can not only halt but also reverse the 'inescapable' metamorphosis into stiff-jointed old age—and that is the really good news.

Raise and lower your arms again. Sense on the repetition of this gesture the flexibility of your joints and muscles. Now say to yourself, or better still, say aloud, "I feel loose and agile; I feel light and free." Raise and lower your arms once more, noticing the ease of the accomplishment. Now say, either to yourself or aloud, "I feel heavy, I feel tense and knotted up." Lift and lower your arms, comparing the movement now. You will notice that your arms have truly become heavier, your shoulders tense.

The point here is that mobility and effort follow your thoughts, motivation, and self-confidence. The anticipation of knots and gnarls is, sorry to say, more often seen in everyday life than lightness and ease: "Life is hard...a pain in the neck. I have a difficult life." Recently I heard someone say, " I have a difficult weekend coming up; I just don't know how I'll get through it." No sooner said and the body is already programmed to expect it. If we assume a time of trial is coming in the days ahead, it makes more sense to say, "I will meet these challenges with a spring in my step and will master them with ease and swiftness." Amazing progress can be made without additional training if we are attentive to the power our thoughts can pass on to the body.

The Movement in Your Mind: MSM

We will now look at a form of imagery used by successful athletes and dancers, one that is also effective for health, beauty, and postural alignment. This technique is known as mental rehearsal and is also called 'mental simulation of movement,' or MSM. In MSM, a bodily movement is imagined without physically performing it. You can experience for yourself the benefits of this technique in the following example.

Lifting the arms with ease

Stand tall with arms relaxed at your sides. Raise and lower both arms. Concentrate on the right arm (or the left if you prefer) and imagine lifting the arm in front of you until it is overhead. Inwardly feel the movement as if you were doing it. Sense the progress of joints and muscles, perhaps even of air flowing past your fingertips. With full concentration and awareness, imagine the movement three more times.

You can make the MSM more vivid by imagining the arm to be a feather or balloon. Mentally lift and lower the arm seven times, then compare how both arms feel.

You will be more aware of the arm you lifted with MSM, even though it was not actively moved. The arm will feel longer, a sign of muscular relaxation. Lift the same arm in actuality and note its lightness. Lift the other arm, the one to which MSM was not applied, to compare it. Note that in comparison it is heavier. Raise both arms together, observing that the practiced arm moves more easily in the shoulder joint. You can feel this best by moving the arms in their overhead position somewhat still further to the back.

What does mental simulation of movement (MSM) do?

MSM relaxes, makes movement lighter and easier, and improves muscular flexibility. Without any movement at all we can train and rejuvenate our bodies. Why would anyone want to do such a thing in the first place? There are several reasons.

In MSM the body receives a workout when physical exertion is not possible, when traveling in a train or an airplane, for instance, or in the case of an injury. MSM is very helpful in regaining strength and flexibility.

MSM can pre-program muscles so that better-coordinated and more precise movement can be achieved, thus encouraging greater efficiency of the loco-motor system and extending the life of joints and muscles.

MSM facilitates learning movement patterns.

MSM conveys to the person practicing it the experience of mobility without strain. In contrast, actively forcing a stretch when one is not flexible produces the sensation of inflexibility, which is detrimental to motivation.

With MSM it is possible to learn a movement from watching another person. This is often used in dance training and is also a valuable tool in everyday life. When we see a person who moves with ease sit down or stand up, we can pick up some of the same facility just by watching it. When we watch movement that appeals to us, it is possible to enhance our own qualities.

How is MSM most effectively applied?

There are several rules for using MSM effectively:

The imagined movement should correspond in speed and rhythm as closely as possible to the actual movement. Practicing a fast movement slowly is not as effective as at its natural speed. If you want to dance with more fullness and elegance, you can prepare by playing aloud the music that goes with the dance, imagining how it feels to dance to it.

Envision the successful completion of a movement. If, for instance, you want to play better golf, feel the swing correctly and see the ball dropping into the hole.

Sense a movement 'from within,' feeling it as if you were actually doing it, rather than from the outside, as if watching yourself in a film.

Practice the simulation at least three or four times.

If you would like to achieve results more quickly, practice three times a day. For instance, if you would like to recapture something of the spinal flexibility you had in your youth, mentally simulate three times a day all movement directions the spine is capable of: forward, backward, sideways and in rotation. This spares the back itself while actually increasing its mobility.

The posture you assume for practicing should be similar to the posture of the actual movement. For example, for the trampoline mentally practice from a slightly teetering standing position rather than from a recumbent position of ease. (Lying down makes imagining the jump more difficult.)

Ideally, the environment where you will practice should likewise be imagined. To prepare for giving a lecture, see and hear the audience at the same time as you practice your text and body posture.

You can also simulate hearing what you will say to yourself during practice.

Intuitive Imagery

This book contains many suggestions for images you can use and how to use them. However, if you discover (that is, create) images for yourself, it is especially helpful because these ideas, thoughts, and pictures are custom-made messages from your own body. Accordingly, in learning to use imagery, a distinction is made between 'programmed' and 'intuitive' images. Programmed images are those taken from a program of some sort—this book, for example. Intuitive images are those that arise spontaneously, often surfacing when least expected. You can encourage this by posing specific questions to yourself. If you are in good health, these questions can help you find imagery to better an athletic achievement or to improve your fitness, appearance, and flexibility.

Suppose you have pain, an injury, or illness, and have been to the doctor for help. Alongside any recommended medical treatment, you can speed your return to health through work with the imagination. It is free of cost and always available. Perhaps you have found that none of the images or mental formulas are working. In this instance, silently ask your body, or whichever part of your body is involved, "What, dear shoulder, (or back, hip joint, knee) is troubling you? What is the source of your problem and what can I do to help?" After asking this question, listen attentively. The answer may appear in words, or as a feeling or image. Sometimes patience is needed and the question to be repeated over several days. The first response is often a clear visual picture of the troubled area in a symbolic form. At this point ask, "And what images can I use to ease the situation, to solve the problem?" Images will emerge to show methods for resolving the pain or other physical circumstance. The images are often of a surprising nature.

An example of how you can free the shoulder

The following is an example from my own experience that may help you to understand better the process of intuitive imagery. When teaching, I have to travel frequently. More often than not, I have to pull my rather weighty bags through train stations and airports. One day when traveling, a pronounced twinge appeared in my shoulder. Over the next several days the pain increased until I was unable to lift my arm. A typical work-related overuse injury had developed. I was thus not quite a poster-perfect example—flexible and fit, a vision of rejuvenation—of what I was teaching! Ointments and compresses had no effect, and as I could not move my arm, I was unable to carry out any therapeutic exercises.

None of the images I was familiar with for shoulder problems brought much relief. As a 'specialist' in this area, this was particularly disappointing to me. So I began a dialogue with my shoulder by asking, "What is wrong, where is this problem coming from? What can I do to help you; I need you mobile, dear shoulder!" A picture emerged: I saw a tangle of seaweed knotted around my shoulder. It looked like a ship's propeller strangled with kelp. Naturally, movement was impossible. I began carefully to clear away the kelp and seaweed, to unwind the mass from my shoulder.

After the seaweed was cleared away, I saw that the shoulder needed care. The muscles needed relaxing and the tendons needed lubrication. In my

*4. Unwinding seaweed
from the shoulder*

imagination I oiled them, sometimes with Vaseline, sometimes with olive oil. Crossing the shoulder joint is a tendon sheath, a sort of tube that surrounds the tendon of the long head of the biceps muscle. I imagined this tube becoming wider to make room for the tendon lying within it, which I continued to rub with lubricant.

I visualized the tendon cells generating lubricant and the tendon feeling elastic and mobile. I imagined that my arm could lift and that the movement felt wonderful (see MSM).

I imagined the process again, whenever I had time, several times daily. After three days my shoulder was mobile and pain free. Previously, such pain had lasted a week.

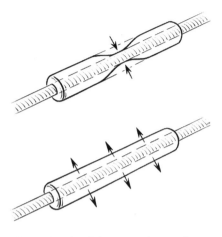

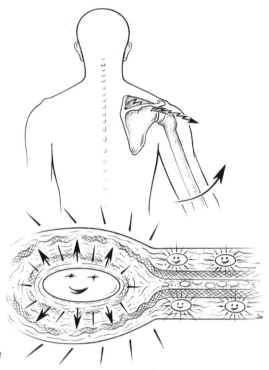

5. The tendon sheath loosens and expands

6. Happy cells in the tendon

Unproven fantasy?

Skeptics might now retort, "These supposed abilities are simply unproven fantasy." Today this statement cannot be supported. All the published research on the subject and the regular appearance of new findings are available to the public. These attest to the power of imagery and expectation in alleviating and even healing illness. Naturally we need reassurance that we can actually contribute to our own health and abilities. Often this assurance is jarred by skepticism, opposing medical assessment, or chronic pain. It should also be remembered that we are not dealing with pills or surgical evaluations but with a very conservative method purely for the mind.

Summing up the practice of intuitive imagery

We will now summarize the use of intuitive imagery:

Positive belief and expectations: I can contribute to my own recovery, healing, and healthy aging. My thoughts and inner imagery have the power to help.

Concentration: I am mindful and focused.

Relaxation and patience: I have a relaxed body and mind as I await the inner dialogue.

I ask my body for an image showing the source of a problem and then for an image showing a solution to it. I revisit the imaged solutions until the problem is alleviated.

It is best to begin with somewhat simple problems: "Today, how might I be more relaxed in sitting, walking, breathing?" With practice and experience, larger challenges can then be ventured.

Conversing with Ourselves

As we have established, the body responds to our thoughts and aspirations; it not only responds but does so continuously. This is a kind of ongoing training and by daily providing the body with precisely defined images of health, we allow this program to unfold. **It cannot be bad advice to devote a portion of our some 40,000 thoughts per day to well-being.**

Prayer is a well-known form of positive self-expression. Prayer can be directed to God alone or expressed as a petition for help, such as in times of illness. This might be for oneself or on behalf of others. Certainly religion is not usually associated with science, but there do exist many studies attesting to the effectiveness of prayer on health.

The first step is to let the body know that we want to communicate with it and that we will do this directly rather than through an external agent. By external agent I mean the suggestions we pick up from the health food, fitness, or beauty industries, and then convey to our body. We could only know if a suggestion for the needs of our individual body type were correct if the body could express its own opinion on the matter and we in turn take note of that opinion.

Beginning the inner dialogue

To begin, say to yourself, "My body hears my thoughts clearly, my body responds to my inner picture of wellness. My muscles sense my thoughts, my joints sense my thoughts, my organs sense my thoughts."

Then ask yourself regularly, "Which thoughts and images are the best and most healthy for my individual body?"

Now confirm the body's response to your thoughts and images. Initially you might feel very little. With time, however, you will feel that reactions are increasingly more exact, as depicted in examples on the subject of motivation and MSM. What possibly begins as a hesitant discourse transforms itself into the kind of tangible dialogue that will set most people on the path to finding effective images and sensations.

Finally, do not give up if a clear answer does not appear immediately. With practice, helpful thoughts and images will indeed arise spontaneously.

Negative-stop, positive-go

What is next? I suggest establishing the practice of a positive inner dialogue also called *self-talk* in sports mental skills training. The first task here is learning how to stop at will unhelpful thoughts and images. Whenever negative inner voices install themselves in your brain, whether in daily life, or in sports or any other specialized activity, the following approach is helpful:

Say to yourself, "Stop."

Consider your actual goal for the body. (Health, beauty, fitness, weight loss…)

Reflect on how you would like to feel about yourself. (Fit, flexible, calm, attractive…)

Resume working with your chosen thought, image, or objective.

Effectively putting it together

Imagery and self-talk function best when they are *embodied*. Embodied means that they can be perceived and their effects can be felt. This occurs most often when imagery and self-conversation have personal meaning, when depiction and language are vibrant, and when positive emotions are involved.

The more we experience our self-talk as an event originating in the physical self, formulated in the cells even, the more effective it is. Cells, after all—brain cells to be exact—are what allow us to converse with our bodies in this way. The process we are exploring uses a kind of echo principle: when we feel the body's echo in response to our imagery or self-conversation, we have created an effective link.

The rule of thumb runs like this: "X (name of the applicable body tissue) radiates love, health, and beauty."

Love, health, and beauty are intended here to contrast with illness and degeneration. If it is possible to penetrate body tissue with the concepts of love and beauty, or even better, to initiate such feelings from body tissue itself, astonishing changes are possible. Unfortunately, few people are familiar with these seemingly simple methods, because from the start they have rejected these as impossible or too facile, and because such people either do not either practice long enough or do not embody the image.

In order to learn how we might best conduct an effective inner dialogue, we will look at our joints, which ideally function with efficiency for a lifetime. The degeneration of cartilage (the smooth covering of bone surfaces in joints is a type of cartilage) is for many an indication of old age, although in actuality it is not. Scientifically speaking, there is no direct link between age and cartilage degeneration. It is of course true that the structure of body tissue changes with age, but the main reason for degeneration lies elsewhere. Cartilage degenerates more in older than in younger people because older people have lived with bad posture over a longer time, and perhaps have also been inactive or have moved incorrectly for longer than a young person. The problem lies for the most part in chronic physical strain from inactivity.

I also know many dancers with cartilage problems, the result of overuse from poor training. What joints appreciate is regular activity within their full range of movement, including moments of compression (within a range) and decompression (which allows the nourishing joint fluid to circulate).

Self-conversation should ideally be phrased as if expressed by the relevant tissue itself, as if the cells of this tissue were making the statement.

When I say to myself, "My cartilage radiates strength and resilience," I am attempting to envision the statement as originating from the cartilage itself, this protective tissue found in all but a few joints. Using this approach we can be more accurate. We can use, for example, images of the cartilage itself in thinking of the knee.

It is often felt, especially if the relevant area has a problem, that the process is not really working, not fulfilling its objective. At times like this we should not give up, but practice again over the following days. (Further exercises for healthy joints can be found in Chapters 3 and 4.)

The following exercises should be performed for five minutes every day and more often if you can find a free moment. These do occur if you look for them: waiting for a train or bus, standing in line at the post office, and so on. Delays lend themselves conveniently to 'health and beauty exercises.'

Is it not rather gratifying that waiting, which we all must do from time to time, can be used to such good purpose?

Over the next few pages you will find an extensive list of statements or affirmations to say to yourself. If you experience a physical response while doing this—relaxation, deeper breathing, a release in a muscle or joint—stay with this particular image a bit longer, repeating it two or three times. The affirmations are formulated to sound as if originating from the body. The affirmation "I'm healthy to the core" or "I am fit and beautiful" can also be a quick defense against statements like "That isn't really so; actually I feel wretched and I am certainly not fit." To turn such thoughts around we will begin with an assertion about the body that encompasses aspirations and goals like fitness, health, and beauty. I have added the word 'love', because it is a healing word and because the attractiveness of those who radiate a sense of love is enhanced. This is common knowledge to all who are, or have ever been, in love. There is no scientific proof, no experimental evidence, verifying that love exists. Yet it clearly does, even for scientists. Initially the expressions may seem peculiar, even self-indulgent, especially if they are foreign to the way you usually think. I recommend simply to keep going; there will come a time when you are accustomed to the language and begin to feel its good effects.

Inner thoughts for health, love, and beauty

Make yourself comfortable and say inwardly:

"I radiate health, love, and beauty from my feelings and throughout my entire body."

"I radiate health, love, and beauty from my very cells."

"I radiate health, love, and beauty from all my tissues."

"I radiate health, love, and beauty from all my organs."

"I radiate health, love, and beauty from my connective tissue."

"I radiate health, love, and beauty from my cartilage."

"I radiate health, love, and beauty from my ankles."

"I radiate health, love, and beauty from my knees."

"I radiate health, love, and beauty from my hip joints."

"I radiate health, love, and beauty from the cartilage in my pelvic joints."

"I radiate health, love, and beauty from the cartilage in my spinal joints."

"I radiate health, love, and beauty from my vertebral discs."

"I radiate health, love, and beauty from the cartilage in my shoulder joints."

"I radiate health, love, and beauty from the cartilage in my arm joints."

"I radiate health, love, and beauty from the cartilage in my hand joints."

"I radiate health, love, and beauty from the cartilage in my jaw."

"I radiate health, love, and beauty from all my tendons."

"I radiate health, love, and beauty from my ligaments."

"I radiate health, love, and beauty from the ligaments in my knee."

"I radiate health, love, and beauty from the ligaments in my spinal column."

"I radiate health, love, and beauty from my skin."

"I radiate health, love, and beauty from my face."

"I radiate health, love, and beauty from all my body's actions."

"I radiate health, love, and beauty from my digestion."

"I radiate health, love, and beauty from my heartbeat."

"I radiate health, love, and beauty from my breathing."

"I radiate health, love, and beauty from my nerve impulses."

"I radiate health, love, and beauty from my thoughts."

"I radiate health, love, and beauty from my movement."

Well-being, joy, and suppleness

You can enhance the expressions above with words such as well being, bliss, suppleness, and joy. Naturally you may also use words of your own choosing.

"I radiate health, beauty, and suppleness from all my body's activities."

"I radiate health, beauty, and well-being from my digestion."

"I radiate health, beauty, and happiness from my heartbeat."

"I radiate health, beauty, and well-being from my breathing."

"I radiate health, beauty, and joy from my nerve impulses."

"I radiate health, beauty, and happiness from my thoughts."

"I radiate health, beauty, and well-being from my movement."

The spa of everyday life

As we have seen, it is interesting to transform certain mundane and possibly obligatory activities into exercises for health and beauty. This includes all common everyday movement, particularly walking, breathing, and sitting. Some examples follow; these can be employed when you next go for a walk.

"With every step I radiate beauty."

"My arms are swinging me to health."

"My legs are striding me to health."

"My joints are massaged with every step."

"With every step I generate more beauty. With every step I generate more health."

"With every step I radiate health and beauty."

"With every step I radiate health."

Resistance and the "but…" challenge

If you notice that you are feeling uncomfortable with positive self-dialogue, the following may be the root cause: resistance to believing that you can truly change and move toward your health and beauty goals. If you think "with every step I radiate health and beauty," and you would really like to add, "but this is never going to work, not for me, I have always had back problems…etc.," then you are experiencing resistance. The problem with resistance is that it is your actual imagery practice. Your foundational imagery is what you believe about your self and your future. If your body image and the image you carry about your potential to change is negative, then no amount of superficial imaging or self-dialogue will really change much.

Try this: lift and lower your arms and notice how it feels to do that. Now think: "I am wrong, something is not good enough about me, I am stuck with the way I am" and lift your arms again. You will feel tension and resistance. Lift your arms once more saying: "I am now moving forward to health and beauty," and notice how it feels. No doubt it will feel a lot easier.

The key is to seek out all resistance and face it squarely. It is easy to do: as soon as it does not feel natural to make positive statements there is a "but…" lurking at the back of your mind. Once the resistance is apparent, there are a variety of ways to remove it. Imagine standing under a shower and feel all the resistance being washed away. Imagine exhaling all resistance and inhaling progress and health. Inwardly say the words 'progress' and 'health' as you inhale. You can also pack all the resistances and buts into a box and imagine them being sent to outer space in a rocket. Be imaginative about letting go of resistance: the combination of focusing on what you would like to experience, and eliminating resistance is very powerful. It is a question of statistics. You process thousands of thoughts and images every day; if you can have more of them focusing on what you would like to be, you will magnetically attract that state into your life.

Scouring the frying pan is a wholesome activity

One evening I was scouring the burned remains from a frying pan. My thoughts about this were, "It hardly delights me to do this. What a nasty odor. It's taking forever! Boring. Yuk...!"

As I was contemplating how much muscle power was needed to vanquish the crust, I said to myself, "This is a great opportunity to turn an annoying chore into something constructive." And I began to say to myself, "With strength and resilience my arm muscles win the day. My fingers curl with elegance and agility. The steam glosses my face and freshens my skin." And with such thoughts I continued. All at once the work was quite relaxing. I was in a good mood doing this washing up, you could even say in cheerful high spirits. A novelty for me!

This short tale is possibly amusing and is also a realistic example of how to create exercises for strength and beauty from everyday activities. Of course sometimes it may also be possible to delegate the more unpleasant tasks in life to someone else and to avoid understandably displeasing activities. In an agreeable situation, a positive inner dialogue, however, is not a major under-taking as mental powers are best developed through challenges: the athlete in the stadium must produce a superlative performance despite numerous distractions. The expectations of trainers and the anticipation of spectators are at fever pitch. The crowd roars in the background; retreat is not an op-tion. Relaxed intensity and optimal preparedness are the order of the day.

A remark in closing: if you are guessing that I have developed a love of kitchen chores, you are mistaken! However, when aggravating situations occur, I do look for a way to create a constructive experience from them.

Chapter 2: The Face

Speaking Can Be a Face-lift

I believe that little persuasive ability is needed to convince people that a person who speaks in loving words has a more beautiful face than a person who does not. Speaking can create beauty and it can create ugliness. To use speech as a positive is our objective.

Any sentence can act as a face-lift. Observe your face and body while you say out loud, "I am fortunate. I am happy. I am having fun." And now say, "I am depressed, I am angry, everything disgusts me." Notice your face this time: you will have noticed the difference, both in your face and in your entire body. A joyful statement 'lifts' the face, making it friendly, attractive, and smoothing out wrinkles. A negative statement pulls the face downward and creates wrinkles. A long chain of negative assertions will inevitably leave such evidence in its wake.

Children hear such things in fairy tales: "Here is the beautiful prince or princess, who thinks only good thoughts and acts in a like manner. Over there slinks the evil witch or sorcerer, with a face to match." Our faces are in a tug-of-war, a 'magnetic field,' between the beautiful princess/prince and the wicked witch or sorcerer. In speaking, we can convey one or the other.

Sharing compliments

Let us close our eyes and imagine the next day's events. On this day we will pass out many compliments. We shall imagine saying something nice to each person we meet. This does both them and us good. What quality of feeling is present after this exercise?

Seduction by voice

Everyone has experienced how seductive a voice can be. Radio and television announcers are mostly chosen for this decisive factor. We hear the voice of the man or woman on the radio and picture an attractive person—one more example of how imagination is present in everyday life.

Like the keen experimentalists we are, let us try, the next time we hear an attractive voice, to imagine an ugly person. We will see that it is difficult. The voice is an important ingredient in our charisma. Small wonder that singers are generally considered attractive, even beautiful, though their outward appearance is not always so.

The echo of my own voice

I imagine people reacting to my voice. I suggest to myself that when people hear my voice, they see before them a lovely picture; they visualize an attractive and charming person.

As an example, suppose we say, "Good morning, did you sleep well?" Now with the same wording, but just beforehand, we say to ourselves, "My voice is beautiful." Then we say again, "Good morning, did you sleep well?" How does the same question feel now?

We'll try it with another statement: "It is a gorgeous day today." We say to ourselves, "My voice is charming and harmonious," and again out loud, "It is a gorgeous day today." How does the statement feel now? Was the voice higher, deeper, or at the same pitch? How do vowels and consonants feel in the mouth and throat?

Creating a beautiful voice

Let us choose a day on which we say to ourselves, "My voice is beautiful" before we speak. This does not mean that we speak haltingly; after a while the inner words will be so quick it will take no time at all to say them. Another idea is to repeat this inner formula and then speak until a natural pause is indicated.

Looking at beauty creates beauty

This experiment is for those days on which you get out of bed on the wrong side. In other words, you don't feel in the best shape, especially mentally. With this exercise though, you can turn things around. The principle is very simple:

Whatever we observe, we note something beautiful in it. We discover in every moment something beautiful, something positive, something constructive. The situations can be completely ordinary, but the process should bring more happiness than before. Here are some examples:

Light reflects beautifully on a windowpane.

A pen has beautifully colored ink.

Someone has especially lovely eyes.

Snow swirls about lightly and drifts downward.

My feet feel warm and cozy in these slippers.

Continue to select positive aspects of sight and sensation, working with them in the above manner to enhance their positive nature. If we make this meaningful, we shall also begin to feel more positively about ourselves. Furthering this inner/outer partnership brings an experience rich in possibility.

People are especially kind to me today.

The wind is cold, but very refreshing.

Today there was good news on the radio.

The effects will be astonishing. At one and the same time you, yourself, are the subject of the same beauty you just discovered by observation. What you see as beautiful will be reflected back to you in a like manner.

Rejuvenating the Face

I once discussed with my students the interesting phenomenon of 'problem zones.' We reflected on what these were and on their effects.

I asked several people, "Which are your problem zones today?" Everyone looked accusingly at his or her thighs and belly. Could the problem originate in the thighs? Or is the problem more than anything in the head? Anyway, whoever defined what a problem zone actually is? What today is considered a problem was, two hundred years ago, considered an asset. So why not use the expression 'beauty zone'? It is my opinion that we should have ever more zones of beauty than of problems, until the beauty zones push away the problem zones.

Facial lines, freckles, and other skin conditions dismay many people. This attitude by itself produces lines and wrinkles. A cure, both for wrinkles and for the cardiovascular system too, takes place when—as a study of 3,300 men and women showed—anger is turned into laughter. Therefore, the following exercises should be fun, with the added bonus of also being funny, which enhances their effectiveness. Smiling and laughing are known to produce endorphins that produce feelings of relaxation and well-being; these in turn smooth facial lines and wrinkles. As an added bonus, laughter burns off calories at a rate approaching aerobic excercise. Laugh your way to your ideal weight!

The miracle of the skin

The skin is the largest organ in the body, a protective barrier that envelops it entirely. It protects us from dehydration and limits invasion of bacteria, viruses, and fungi. The skin guards us from the sun and from other external stresses like injurious contact with the palms of the hands and soles of the feet. The skin helps to regulate body temperature, is an important sensory organ, transmits touch stimuli, and in facial expressions is a medium of communication. In short, the skin is a work of wonder of much diversity that looks after us with great care.

So how is it that relaxation makes you beautiful? Relaxation allows the tissues of skin and muscle to regenerate and to be more plentifully supplied with blood. A fresh, youthful appearance is thereby encouraged. A relaxed face is a beautiful face, the thought of which will now motivate us to release the separate facial areas.

Relaxation makes you beautiful

My facial muscles are relaxed and calm. My facial muscles are released and refreshed. My skin is relaxed and calm. My skin is released and refreshed.

My lips are relaxed and calm. My lips are released and refreshed. I sense my breathing in my lips. My lips become filled with oxygen.

The muscles surrounding my eyes are relaxed. My eye muscles are released and refreshed. I sense my breathing in my eye muscles and they are filled with oxygen.

My eyes are relaxed and calm. My eyes are released and refreshed. My eyelids are relaxed and calm. My eyelids are released and refreshed.

Wrinkles around the eyes

One day you wake up and notice in the mirror that you have (more) wrinkles around the eyes. What you then say to yourself is not very positive: "Wrinkles already?"; "Surely more wrinkles than yesterday! What happened? I'm gray and falling apart!" And thus negative mental training is enthusiastically resumed.

An emotionally charged vision of the future sends a strong message to the body. The mental picture of facial lines gets a lot of brainpower and accordingly will be tracked down and urged to vacate. It might, however, be better to think less about "no wrinkles" than about the skin we would like to have. With this in mind, a list of desirable qualities for the skin might be: smooth, radiant, youthful, fresh, bright, attractive...

Add your own wishes to this list. Feel the skin on your face by gliding your hand softly over it. While doing this, say to yourself the words you have chosen from your wish list. Practice this 'complexion wish list' three times a day, or any time you feel like it or catch negative thoughts trying to sneak back in.

Smoothing facial lines lifts the spirits

Probably you have smoothed a freshly laid tablecloth with your hand. This is another image we can use to smooth out facial lines. We imagine the skin being smoothed from the middle of the forehead to the temples. To enhance the sensation we can use the hand, gliding the fingers slowly outward. We shall repeat this movement three times, and then move to the skin beneath the eyes. With the fingertips we shall stroke outward and imagine the skin becoming like silk. As your fingers glide over your skin, clearly visualize the skin becoming smooth, and watch wrinkles flattening out and disappearing. It is most effective if we can see the actual transformation from wrinkle to smooth skin. We shall repeat the finger stroke three times for each area.

Now let's smooth the skin over the mouth with the help of our imagination and a gentle movement of the fingers. Gently hold the corners of your mouth and give them a slight stretch by moving your fingers away from each other. Imagine your lips smoothing and plumping up. Watch the changes to your mouth with your inner eye and think the words 'smooth,' 'beautiful lips,' or whatever you would like to add. It is likely that your skin will feel more firm and smooth, your entire body will be more relaxed, and you will be in good spirits.

A face-lift without Botox®

For this, we'll rub our palms against each other and feel the energy between our hands. Now we'll lay our hands on our face and imagine each skin cell drifting up-ward. The cells are light and float like small balloons. Think the words 'calm and beautiful skin.' After about two minutes, we'll take our hands off and see how our face feels. It is lighter, brighter, and buoyant. If you have any resistance to this feeling, seek it out and send it away.

Dry skin can be helped with imagery and movement. When we drink enough water, it may circulate throughout the body but is perhaps not sufficiently available to our facial skin. A cell is made primarily of water and is itself bathed in extra-cellular fluid, the fluid found around all cells. Cells also produce water as a by-product of energy generation.

Directing moisture to the face

Let us imagine that increased moisture will be directed to the face. Place your hands on your face and gently vibrate your lower arms and hands, imagining that the cells are attracting moisture. Certain cells will become plump with moisture and the extra-cellular fluid will circulate freely. This will give the face a new and youthful freshness.

Tension is your body arguing with itself—it is excess power that is not being directed toward meaningful activity. Instead, it blocks your movement, and causes your muscles to be tight and your skin to wrinkle.

Tension is commonly located in your neck. If your neck is tense, it will show in your face. The good news is that you can rapidly release neck tension with the following procedure:

Releasing neck tension to relax the face

Place the palm of one hand on your neck and the other hand on top of the first hand. Now gently squeeze your neck using both hands. Imagine that you are 'juicing' your neck, squeezing all tension out of it as if the muscles were a sponge and that you are squeezing water out of it. With your hands still holding your neck muscles, gently nod your head forward and back as if you are saying "yes-yes." Now slowly let go of your grip and imagine fresh fluid entering the muscle cells and tissues in the neck. Experience the muscle as a sponge that is expanding and taking all the space for itself. Repeat the procedure one more time, 'squeeze-nod-release,' remove your hands, and enjoy the sensation of a relaxed and lengthened neck. Also notice the change in your facial expression.

Living Connective Tissue

Below the epidermis (outer layer) of the skin is an elastic framework of connective tissue proteins, called *collagen* and *elastin*. Collagen is the most abundant protein in the body and varies in thickness and consistency. One of the results of overexposure to the sun is collagen damage.

Fibroblasts are the cells responsible for the production of collagen. Touch, light massage, and imagery can activate these cells. Facial massage stimulates fibroblasts to produce collagen and other integumentary (skin) proteins. We will imagine the skin as a fragrant meadow carpeted in flowers.

We can see in the illustration that the many connective tissue cells produce plenty of collagen. The collagen framework of the skin is strong and flexible.

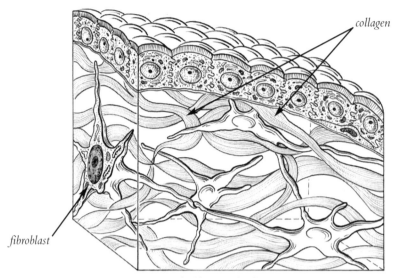

7. Fibroblasts and collagen

A decrease in elasticity, the formation of wrinkles, and a sagging appearance, have nothing to do with gravity. Gravity inevitably pulls the skin downward, but it is the loss of fat in the deepest layer of the skin, the hypodermis, that causes these conditions. The adipose (fat) cells located here serve as an energy reserve and a layer of insulation. When fat in the hypodermis decreases, the skin becomes too thin and begins to sag and fold.

Fat for a more beautiful skin

Let us imagine the deep layers of our skin that are well supplied with fat creating much of the skin's strength and resilience. Let us sense how the fat cells in our skin lift and smooth out from below. Let us picture how plump the fat cells are and how strong and supportive the collagen. If the word 'fat' carries a negative connotation for you, eliminate this resistance since in the case of skin, fat is a good thing.

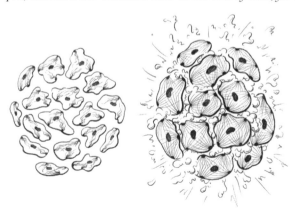

8. Left, cells with little; right, cells with abundant fat and collagen

Young children believe in fairies, adults do not usually. Yet *The Lord of the Rings* is one of the most successful books and films of all time. Fantasy is fascinating; we identify ourselves with it. Heroes and heroines, fairies and elves animate us in the same way, and can serve as a good technique for imagery.

9. Beauty spirits circle the face like small angels

The beauty spirits

In this exercise we shall imagine little spirits flying about us, sprinkling health-dust or health-wishes, like the fairy Tinker Bell in Peter Pan. The spirits might also have small wands with which they sprinkle wellness-magic.

Let us begin with the feet, feeling the spirits circling our legs and continuing up and around from all sides, sending magic sparkles of health glittering all over the body. The spirits will then move to our face and conscientiously do everything needed to give our skin a beautiful, smooth, and fresh appearance. Our face will be anointed with the best salves and fine-tuned with the most beautiful glow.

Activating the Stem Cells

To accomplish the diverse tasks of the body, 250 different types of cells have evolved. These cells all originate from a fertilized egg cell, or *ovum*. Through continual cellular specialization and divisions numerous beyond imagining, the body's different tissues are produced. Once a tissue is established, the cells quickly become embedded and are capable of little movement. The original cell of a tissue though, *in embryo*, is able to move about freely. Such cells are piloted to their target destination with help from auxiliary cells and chemical 'landing lights.' Once the cell arrives at the correct location, it begins life *in situ* ('in place') as a tissue. Metabolism (the sum of chemical changes taking place in tissue) rather than movement is now its main purpose. Blood, however, is a fluid tissue and its cells remain movable for their entire lives.

Certain cells do not differentiate and thus remain immature. These are called stem cells and they are active near their origin. When stem cells divide, they produce one cell that is an exact copy of themselves (so that they never become extinct) and another that is a tissue type. The immortality of stem cells is fascinating. If we could activate the stem cells for every tissue, it would seem as if 'eternal youth' were truly beckoning. A *pluripotent* stem cell is one that begets offspring capable of different functions. Depending on the tissue, stem cells are either very active or apparently disappear. Blood contains pluripotent stem cells that produce its five typical cells. These stem cells are found in bone marrow. Radioactive rays can damage stem cells. But if all the stem cells in a mouse are killed by radioactivity and replaced with only twenty new stem cells, the mouse can regenerate its blood and live on, in mouse terms, to a ripe old age.

Within the deepest layer of skin are the stem cells that continually renew it. Too much radiation (from the sun, for example) will damage the stem cells and thus age the skin more quickly.

The inner wall of the intestine is rebuilt daily. Approximately nine ounces, nearly half a pound of cells, will be secreted every day from the tips of the *villi*. (The villi are finger-like projections in the intestinal lumen that increase its area of absorption.) The intestine is thus prepared anew each day for the absorption of nutrients. This process is hindered by a diet that clogs or blocks it. In this instance we age faster, because we are poorly nourished, even if we are taking in sufficient nutrients.

Cell cleansing as rebirth

Let us imagine that some cells and their surrounding area, called the cell matrix, are taking a bath. They will be scrubbed from top to bottom. All debris and waste products will be washed away. This may need some persistence, as all the old layers must be peeled off. We can see the waste-water flowing out of the cells. There is a drain right at the bottom of the cell through which everything flows that our body disposes of: all types of grime, bad nutritional habits, and old unhealthy thoughts that have damaged our cells.

Under the crust of debris, something astonishing appears: a bright luminous fresco with wonderful scenes of happiness, peace, and harmony. All the colors of the rainbow dance across this fresco. Golden-clad figures move joyfully about. It is as if we had just unveiled a hidden masterpiece of the Renaissance. It is in the truest sense a re-birth of cells.

An American study showed that stress accelerates the aging of skin many times over. It also showed that stress damages genetic material. At the tips of the chromosomes are small protective caps called *telomeres*, which break down much more quickly under stress. The opposite of stress is "flow", a continuous act of discharge. We flow with the stream of things, rather than swim against them. The body's own fluid in and around the cells can be used to assist this.

Cells relax in a bath

While on a leisurely walk, we visualize the fluid within our cells. With each step, this fluid gently washes to and fro. Using this image we can randomly relax any part of our body. If we consciously picture water moving within the cells, it will bring relaxation directly to the tissues. We also imagine the fluid outside every cell flowing about it like the water in a relaxing bath.

10. Fluid washes in and around the cells

We can practice this with the neck and shoulder. Each step will bring a lovely stream of water to the neck and shoulder cells. After a time these areas will be completely released. We can sense also that the skin cells, above all those in the face, contain streams of water. Let us choose other parts of the body and relax them with this image of flowing cellular fluid.

We can practice this with the neck or with the shoulder. Each step brings a sluice of water into the neck and shoulder cells. After a time these areas are completely released. We sense also that the skin cells, above all those in the face, have actively coursing fluid. We choose further parts of the body and relax them with this image of flowing cellular fluid. In this way we can be active, and our activity be helped to release through "cellular awareness."

Stem cells as fountains of youth

I imagine how my entire body—bone marrow, intestines, even the muscles and nervous system—is an environment for active and healthy stem cells. These stem cells keep my tissues young and healthy. My blood is constantly renewed (at the rate of about one million new blood cells per second), my intestinal walls are renewed, and my entire body is clothed in youthful energy and renewal. In my imagination, at the stem cell level I am reborn, and with fresh tissue I am ever ready for a new start.

Chapter 3: The Joints and Cartilage

Flexible Joints for a Lifetime

A joint is the place where two bones meet to have a discussion, the content of which is partnership in movement. The ends of bones, where the joints are situated, are covered in cartilage and provided with a layer of fluid lubricant. This coating keeps the bone surfaces in healthy condition, allowing them to glide over each other without friction. The manner in which they glide can take many different forms, depending on the type of joint and ligament structure involved. But they all have one thing in common: for efficient movement to take place, the surfaces must fit closely and conform to each other.

Figuratively speaking, our body's flexibility resides in its joints. When the joints are free, our minds are more open to creative ideas. Above all, we are ready to embrace different attitudes; we are not so fixated upon our own opinions. If a joint seizes up or has other problems, we might ask ourselves if something in our life has also seized up or if we have become too set in our ways.

Cartilage and Connective Tissue

At the ends of the bones is a covering of hyaline cartilage, which in healthy condition is whitish, translucent, and smooth. This covering allows the joint to resist pressure and at the same time provide optimal gliding. When healthy, cartilage is very endurable and its surface ensures the nearly frictionless movement of both ends of the bone. When this is not the case, there is either a problem within the joint itself, or there is tension in the overlying muscles and connective tissue structures.

To maintain the health of our cartilage it is important to provide the joint with pressure as well as release from pressure, and a full range of movement at regular intervals. The release of pressure allows the joint space to fill with *synovial fluid* which contains nutrients for the cartilage. Pressure stimulates the growth of cartilage cells and the movement massages the fluid into the cartilage.

A characteristic of connective tissue is that the cells do not lie next to each other but are separated by varying distances. (See Illustration 7.) Connective tissue cells have a type of garden; they are not lined up side by side as are the (epithelial) cells of the skin, but have some free space between them. Despite this separation, connective tissue cells have an intrinsic affinity to each other, because in their gardens vines and climbing plants grow and provide a link to other gardens. The gardens thus share plants and are in contact with and influence each other. If one garden is in trouble, the others quickly become aware. The garden can likewise reciprocate with support and relief. In anatomical language, the area between the connective tissue cells is called the *matrix*.

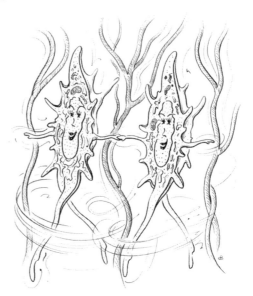

11. Dancing connective tissue cells in their garden of collagen vines

A world without friction

There are days when everything runs smoothly. This is the condition in which our joint cartilage works best, and when we embody their gliding surfaces, our lives function as an illustration of this frictionless world. Should our daily routine, work, or ideas stagnate, it is as if our joints were thirsty. They lack synovial fluid. When there has been a while with 'friction,' it is time to embody synovia. Synovia is the lubricant in the joints, a thin film of fluid spread over the surface of the cartilage. When we move the elbows, for example, the bony ends with their cartilage casings glide over this fluid. Thus our bones never touch each other. We can think of the synovial proteins as small ball bearings. In Illustration 12 we can see this in the example of a hip joint, with the ball bearings much enlarged.

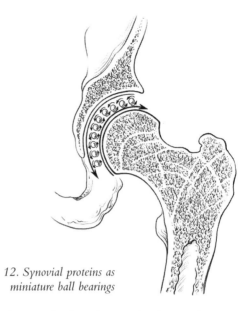

*12. Synovial proteins as
miniature ball bearings*

Healthy joints are always lubricated. If we begin the day with an inner gliding 'joint awareness,' external events adapt to this image. Our inner state causes problematic conditions to melt like butter on warm toast.

The anti-arthritis shower for the joints

Choose a joint and imagine yourself wandering into the joint capsule. The joint capsule is a connective tissue shell that protects and stabilizes the joint. Lining the inside of the joint capsule is the synovial membrane. Within this membrane are the cells that produce synovia, the joint lubricant. When we move a joint, the soft synovial membrane is 'tickled' and its cells release joint lubricant. By moving, we activate a synovia-shower. Our movement and our imaginative powers produce the fluid that lubricates joints and keeps them young and free of friction.

Joints are nourished through bearing and releasing weight. During release, a kind of suction takes place that draws synovial fluid into the joint space. During the subsequent phase of weight bearing, the synovia that is now available in the joint space is massaged into the joint cartilage. With sufficient regular movement, arthritis and other degenerative conditions can be thus averted.

Within the synovial membrane, we also meet countless lymphatic sub-capillaries that remove debris and used-up lubricant. We sense how movement purifies, cleans, and refreshes the joint.

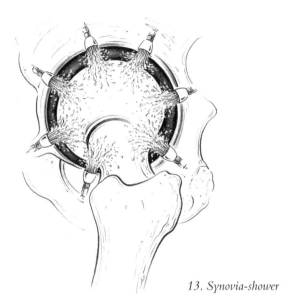

13. Synovia-shower

Because there is a thin film of fluid between the joint cartilages of two bones pushing against each other, we always walk on water, so to speak. When we stand, our pelvis does not sit directly on the thighbone (femur), but on the synovia that lubricates the head of this bone. Our thighbone does not rest directly atop the shinbone (tibia), but on the film of fluid that lies on its meniscus and cartilage. The same goes for the foot. We stand, in a sense, on fluid.

Walking on water

Let us go a few steps further with this thought: we are walking on fluid, on synovia. As soon as we embody this thought, our movement becomes smoother, our breathing more relaxed, and our cartilage better nourished.

Picturing the opposite (bone falling directly upon bone), causes movement to feel rigid, even painful. It is preferable, therefore, to stay with the version that makes us feel flexible and relaxed in movement: the sense of floating on water in every joint.

Arches in your cartilage

To understand other ways we can benefit the joints, it is very helpful to visualize how cartilage is constructed. The *collagen fibrils*, thin threads of collagen within the cartilage, are arranged in an archlike fashion. This is not surprising, as the arch is a sturdy structure capable of supporting extremely heavy loads and used extensively by the Romans in building support structures (See my book *Dynamic Alignment Through Imagery,* listed in about the author at the end of this book). Cartilage, though, has a fluid nature and is not made of stone. Its building material is collagen fibrils surrounded by water.

Developing resilient cartilage arches

Standing upright, imagine the myriad arches of hyaline cartilage supporting you. These arches are very elastic and smooth, and very strong at the same time. Perform small bouncing movements with your legs and imagine the living cartilage arches elastically bending and springing back. Imagine that this loading and unloading of weight strengthens and builds up the cartilage.

Regeneration of cartilage cells

The cells of cartilage are called *chondroblasts* and *chondrocytes*. The elongated chondrocytes are less active than the roundish chondroblasts. Chondroblasts are very active cells, producing collagen and proteins capable of binding to water. These proteins (*glycosaminoglycan* and *proteoglycan*), with help from their strong negative charge, attract and surround themselves with a bound coating of water. This coating enables the cartilage to withstand great pressure. Figuratively speaking, the water-binding proteins are like a combination of sponge and waterbed. On the one hand they are able to attract water like a sponge filling up, while on the other they can hold water like a waterbed. Their actual appearance is rather like the sprouting tendrils of a plant.

As with everything in the microscopic world, these sprouts are very changeable in their form and function. Adhering themselves to collagen fibers to stabilize the tissue, they absorb impact like a buffer and protect against overload. They are very malleable and elastic, like rubber. Bacteria have difficulty invading the thicket of these extensions, as do too-large proteins that do not belong in the area; these are re-absorbed into the vessels.

The vitality of cartilage is maintained by constantly replacing these proteins. In a little over a week, *organelles* (small organs within a cell) in the chondroblasts have caused the proteins to be replaced completely. The tissue ages if this new structure 'dozes off,' and this happens if we don't keep it awake through conscious movement, breathing, and awareness of sensation. Balanced nutrition, with adequate amounts of vitamin-rich fresh foods, also plays a role. However, a healthy diet without movement is not effective in keeping tissue fit.

To function with youthful vim and vigor, cells also require sufficient oxygen. Ideally, physical exercise should be accompanied by conscious breathing. Oxygen and nutrients in the form of glucose and amino acids are transported from bone to cartilage via synovia. A deficient blood supply in bone and insufficient nutrient transport to synovia depletes the fitness of cartilage.

Blood flow to the cartilage frees the joints

In my thoughts one night before going to sleep, I spent some time imaging the bone marrow in my pelvis. I saw a great deal of red marrow, which produces red blood cells. It was a new experience for me, perceiving the marrow and blood supply with such clarity. I thought about the experience, but attached no particular significance to it, and fell asleep.

The next morning, my hip joints felt very elastic and agile; they were more flexible. Stair climbing was no effort; to the contrary, I bounded up stairs with pleasure. Only then did I relate this to my vision of the previous evening. The image apparently enabled a better supply of blood to reach the cartilage. One night was sufficient to bring about an improvement in joint mobility.

A fresh sponge to help arthritis

We can picture the area between cartilage cells (the matrix) as a sponge. To keep the fluid in the sponge fresh, it is necessary to squeeze it out from time to time, so that stale water is rinsed away. When the sponge expands again, fresh, nutrient-rich fluid will be absorbed into it. It should not surprise us to learn that this exchange of fluid takes place through sufficient alternation of weight bearing and release of pressure. If these two states are not balanced, too few nutrients will be absorbed into the cartilage (i.e. sponge) and it will begin to degenerate; the matrix shrinks and can hold less water. The cartilage then loses its ability to resist pressure, and the collagen threads begin to degenerate and develop furrows and cracks. The underlying bone is thus no longer protected and an arthritic condition develops.

In the advanced stages of arthritis, it can be very challenging to exercise sufficiently, because every weight-bearing movement brings pain. For a solution, we look to gentle weight bearing plus Mental Simulation of Movement (see page 13) to stimulate cartilage repair, while at the same time

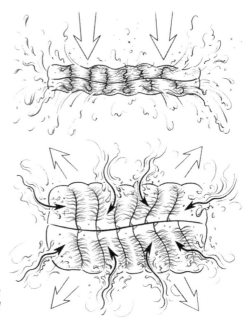

14. Loading and unloading of joint cartilage as sponge and waterbed

causing the least possible pain. Too much pain leads to tension in the tissue, which in turn restricts blood supply.

Ordinary walking is a good example of balanced loading and unloading of weight. As we walk, each time one leg is loaded, the other swings through the air. In the loaded leg the cartilage-sponge is in the compression phase, while in the swinging leg, it is in the absorbent phase. The exchange between compression and expansion of the sponge is fast but dynamic.

For a full transport of nutrients to the cartilage, however, we would need a longer phase of loading and unloading. This happens in many training forms; Hatha yoga is a good example, because phases of exertion alternate with phases of rest. Between yogic poses, a resting phase is always inserted, in which you lie on your back (*Shavasana*, the 'corpse pose') and practice nothing beyond awareness of sensations. Many yoga instructors emphasize that this resting phase is more important than the active pose. For achievement-oriented people, this is difficult to accept. But the cartilage understands perfectly: the resting phase is its opportunity to absorb oxygen and nutrients.

Health Imaging is Always at Hand

I suggest bringing the awareness of loading and unloading the joints into your every day life. Simply being aware of the pressure changes within your body will improve your coordination and posture. To delegate physical awareness to certain limited times during your weekly schedule only goes so far in improving the health of your body. Since you are walking, standing, sitting and lying down daily you can practice the awareness of the joints at any time during the day. Simply replace some of the repetitive thought patterns you have during an average day (about 40,000) with some high quality health imaging and you will start to notice immediate improvements.

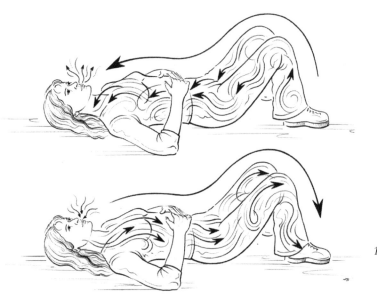

15. Breath flows
through
the body

Resting with imagery

To practice imaging, in a supine position lie on a comfortable mat with the knees bent and your feet on the floor. As this position tends to make the legs fall to either side you can attach a scarf or a soft belt around the thighs, just above the knees. The reason for this outward-falling tendency is tension in the muscles that rotate the legs outward. The arms relax across the chest or at the sides of the body along the floor. Small pillows under the head, under each elbow, and under the balls of the feet, add comfort.

To begin, observe your breathing. Imagine that your inward breath streams downward like a wave, from the bottom of the body to the top. Your outward breath flows upward in the opposite direction. These currents of breath flow through all cells. (See Illustration 15.)

After observing your breath for several minutes, extend your awareness to your physical surroundings, to the place where you are lying. Which parts of your body touch the floor? Which places seem tight, which constricted? Are there areas that feel comfortable and pleasant?

Imagine the posterior side of your body spreading out on the floor. Begin with the soles of the feet spreading like warm honey. The same thing happens in the lower and the upper back. Imagine your back widening, broadening and elongating. The shoulder blades fall downward away from the back, and come to rest on two small clouds.

16. View from below—the posterior side of the body expands

A car wash for the back

Imagine two spools of fluffy wrap-around wash mops, similar to those in an automated carwash, but smaller. These spools release tension from the posterior side of your body. They spiral slowly down the back from the shoulder blades to the pelvis. The outward rolling of the mops expands the back further; the downward spiraling conveys a sense of increasing length. Feelings of spaciousness develop in your back, aided by deep breathing, right into the cells.

Repeat this imagery exercise: Two spools of fluffy wrap-around wash mops move slowly downward along the back. The outward turning of the rolls creates a feeling of breadth and looseness in the back.

To conclude, direct awareness once more to your breathing. The inward breath is like a wave flowing downward through the body from below. The outward breath flows back up in the opposite direction. These breath-waves flow through every cell.

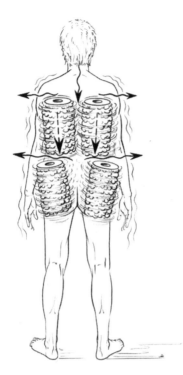

17. *Fluffy wrap-around wash
mops loosen the back*

Muscle tension and cartilage

Tense muscles make life rough for the cartilage. Tense muscles constrict the joint, which accordingly becomes less well nourished. The opposite situation is not ideal either: slack musculature, the product of insufficient physical activity, produces too little pressure and movement to bring synovia to the cartilage. Whether tense or slack, such musculature furthers the development of arthritis in the joint.

Our objective is balanced muscle tonicity. Tense muscles and the connective tissue surrounding them must be released; lax muscles must become activated. Common places in the body that often suffer from tension are the neck, shoulders, lower back, and the area between the shoulder blades. (See *Relax Your Neck, Liberate Your Shoulders,* listed in about the author at the end of this book.)

For many people, inactivity produces musculature that has too little tone in the abdomen and hip area, while muscles in the shoulders and arms (in compensation) show too much tension. What results is a typical pattern of tension from working at a desk.

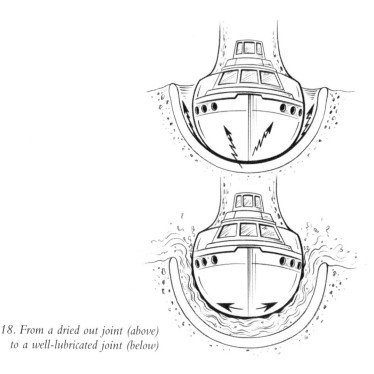

*18. From a dried out joint (above)
to a well-lubricated joint (below)*

Synovial massage

*Begin with joints which, for reasons of inactivity or tension, have become 'dried up.'
Movement and imagery will help right away.*

*Shake the right arm thoroughly for half a minute, while picturing the muscles
falling loosely around the bones. Then allow the arm drop to the side of the body
and shake it lightly. Imagine how the joint space has widened through the movement's gravitational pull on the arm. Lift the arm again and move it with a sense
of power, as if moving your arm under water. Imagine synovia being massaged into
the cartilage as a result.*

*Repeat this process 3 times: shake, then drop the arm to the side, allowing synovia
to be absorbed, and then move with exertion to massage synovia into the cartilage.
Sense how this exercise brings blood to the muscles and to all the tissues. As you
practice, your tissue will be nourished and cleansed of residue.*

Now compare the feeling in both arms by moving them a little and raising
them overhead. The arm that is 'saturated' with synovia feels lighter and
more mobile, the joint more lubricated. The same exercise can naturally be
transferred to joints in the spine, leg, or any other part of the body.

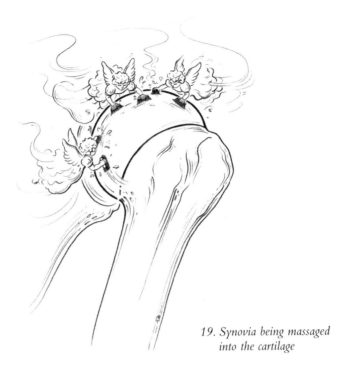

*19. Synovia being massaged
into the cartilage*

Releasing the joints using balls

Because we are not standing on our legs or stabilized by the arms, the movement must be accomplished with help from the torso—controlled by it, so to speak. The torso musculature is strengthened and at the same time the massaging effect of the ball causes muscles and connective tissue to loosen. Rolling on balls is also an ideal balancing exercise, putting minimal weight on the joints. It is therefore appropriate for stimulating nutrient absorption in the joints, and for preventing and possibly even reversing arthritis. (See the exercise and accompanying Illustration 20.)

Rolling on balls for supple joints

Using two Franklin Balls or a Franklin Mini Roller (see Resources at the end of this book), place the balls next to each other, one under each buttock. (The balls should not be too high up or they will cause your back to arch.) Move the pelvis slowly back and forth, sideways, and then in any direction you want. These movements cause oxygen and nutrients to be drawn into the lower back and hip joints.

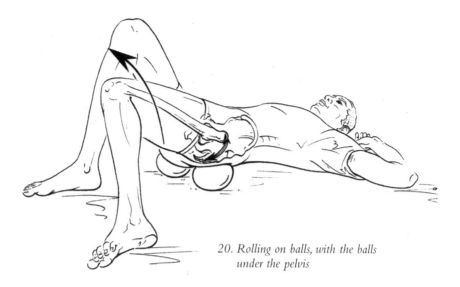

*20. Rolling on balls, with the balls
under the pelvis*

After a few minutes, place one ball under the upper left arm and another under the upper right arm. Stretch the arms out, pull them back in, rotate them to the left and then to the right—or in any way that allows new areas of muscle to be massaged.

Imagine how relaxed the muscles are, how well circulated with blood, and how the cartilage is plentifully supplied with synovia.

Now place the balls under the right and left calves. Stretch out one leg, then the other. Feel the joint spaces opening. Remove the balls and relax with a sense of spaciousness in the joints.

Chapter 4: The Bones

Bones are the longest-lasting human body parts. Skeletal remains are the only direct physical evidence we have of our prehistoric ancestors. These bones reveal the story of the person to whom they once belonged. Was this person male or female? How old was she or he? Was life difficult? What sort of food was eaten? Was the person healthy, diseased, injured? What was the person's posture like and how did this person move? How strong were the muscles, which muscles were used, which were not? This and much more can be determined from bones. We might allow ourselves a somewhat macabre question: what would people in a thousand years see when examining our skeletons? Have we nourished ourselves well and exercised enough; what was our life expectancy?

As previously mentioned, a large part of aging is our attitude toward it. The good news is that we can influence the health of our bones with every breath; we can write the future history of our own bones. Dear reader, the posture that you have assumed right now, while reading this book, influences the very structure of your bones.

An Upright Carriage Keeps Us Young

With advancing age, unfortunately it is the locomotor system that can really get into trouble. The leading causes are physical inactivity, poorly coordinated and tense movement, and misaligned posture. Man is the only being to have adapted an upright posture, which puts humans in a unique position. This has many advantages. The hands are free to function and walking upright is very efficient. No cat or dog can stand or walk for as long as a (normally fit) human. The construction of four-legged animals is like a suspension bridge such as the Golden Gate Bridge in San Francisco. Between the two front and two back pylons is a cable-like span (the spinal column.) Lengthy standing is strenuous for the pylons. Dogs and cats prefer to lie down rather than stand. A human is that same bridge turned ninety degrees to the perpendicular—a brilliant trick with advantageous results, as described above. The human spine, however, boasts a series of counterbalanced arches which create springiness and strength at the same time. The lumbar and neck are the only parts of the spine still in the four-legged animal-Golden Gate Bridge config-uration (*lordosis* or commonly known as 'swayback'.) The other parts in the thorax and sacrum have bent in the opposite direction to create a resilient counterbalancing system called *kyphosis* (*kyphos* meaning 'hump.')

In the reordering of the organs relative to this posture, we are like chim-panzees and orangutans, which led the way. Our common ancestor, rela-tively upright, pulled itself along from branch to branch on long arms. This adaptation in organ placement evolved together with the upright (hanging) posture. In tandem, very mobile shoulders, long arms, and strong abdominal and pelvic floor muscles appeared to ensure that the organs, now pushing down toward the pelvis, were kept close to the center. Consequently, suffi-cient pelvic floor and abdominal strength is very important in humans, and the organs themselves must be kept in good tonicity through proper breathing and regular movement. Organs that lack tone tend to sag down and push against the pelvic floor and abdominal wall, and no amount of su-perficial abdominal training will compensate for a lack of organic strength.

There is, though, a significant difference between humans and great apes in the effect of gravity upon the skeleton. The skeletons of great apes are regularly stretched out, as the animal often dangles from branches, whereas we stand on the ground. This means that our joints and spinal column are compromised by gravity. With good posture and conse-quently balanced spinal curves this is not a problem because good pos-ture requires very little muscle effort to remain upright. We are a balancing tower of bones, so to speak, continually returned to the per-pendicular through minute muscular contractions.

Not so with poor posture: the lopsided tower must use intensive and on-going muscle contractions to prevent itself from toppling over. This pro-duces pain, decreased blood circulation, and excess pressure in muscles, ligaments, and vertebral discs. Even a small improvement in posture will liberate muscles toward increased flexibility. Your flexibility is only as good as your posture permits.

The goal of postural training is efficient and healthy movement. Therefore, placing your body in what may seem to be the correct po-sition through muscular effort is one of the most common mistakes of postural training. Contracted muscles are less available to power your movement, which means that flexibility and economy of movement is lost. Also, a strategy based on conciously holding your body in a cer-tain position vanishes as soon as you stop focusing on it. The most el-egant solution is to improve psosture by becoming aware of healthy function. As soon as you move your pelvis or spine with awareness of good function, posture will immediately improve.

The following key exercises for visualization and balance present good schooling for posture. For those who would like further information, please consult *Dynamic Alignment through Imagery* or attend specialized courses in posture.

Three Types of Bone Cells

There are three main types of bone cells: those that build it, those that take up residence when the bone is ready, and those that break it down again for renewal. The builders are called *osteoblasts*; the residents, *osteocytes*; and the demolition crew, *osteoclasts*.

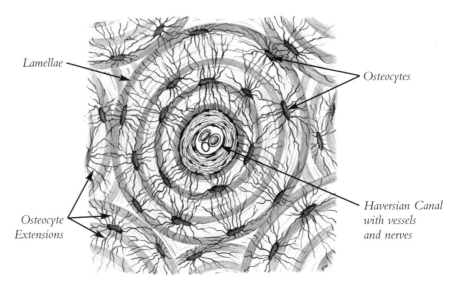

21. Osteocytes—the resident bone cells

Osteoporosis, an abnormal brittleness in bones, is not a disease in itself, but is an imbalance between the building up and breaking down of bone tissue. Osteocytes were originally osteoblasts; as osteocytes they no longer take part in bone building. Osteoclasts, the cells that break down bone, are tunneling machines like those used in road construction, boring their way into the bone to ready it for renewal.

The collective teamwork of the three types of bone cells is influenced by physical activity. The rebuilding of bone can be very quickly altered. Should the bone not be made to bear weight, it will slowly break down or even return to a basic shape. For example, a healthy shinbone in cross section is somewhat triangular. When no longer loaded (such as when placed in a cast) it becomes round, the default shape of a long bone—the bone type to which the shinbone belongs.

Bones are comprised of mineral salts, fluid, and organic matter such as proteins. Should the mineral salts (calcium carbonate and calcium phosphate) be removed, the bone would be almost like a piece of elastic you could tie in a knot. Living bone has therefore both a firm and a flexible component.

Building up the bones

Take an easy stance and feel the weight of the body distributed equally over the legs and feet. Weight acting on bones causes them to build and strengthen. Picture how your body weight stimulates and invigorates the bone. If you bend and straighten your legs, or sway on them, the bone cells become more activated still.

Sit down and notice the release of weight from the legs. Cell activity lessens.

Stand up again and sway on the legs. Imagine the flexible component of bones, which is like rubber. Walk a few steps with the sensation of bone elasticity. Note that with this sensation you walk with more spring and looseness.

Standing on balls to activate bones and improve posture

Balance exercises are an excellent way to stimulate the bones and improve the posture. When we use corrective movements to hold our balance, almost

22. Standing on balls and throwing a ball—coordination and postural training

all the muscles in the body are involved. Gravity exerts its influence on any angle of the body straying from the perpendicular—the ideal exercise for bones. A simple daily walk on rolled bath towels is enough to be beneficial. The deluxe version of this exercise is to stand on two air-filled Franklin Balls. And why not exercise with a partner, including throw-and-catch?

Joint problems—too much friction between bones?

The following example is an exercise for intuitive imagery. John visualizes his knee; he concentrates his thoughts on the knee. The following picture arises: within the joint there is something that looks like sand or grit and causes the joint to get stuck. John asks, "What sort of image might help to solve this problem?"

After several minutes of concentration, the image of a current of water suddenly arises. Water flows through the joint space and washes around the femur, over the top surface of the shinbone, and all through the area beneath the kneecap. This water rinses the sand and grit from the joint; John imagines the grit being completely washed away. Initially the water streaming out is dirty, and then it becomes clearer and cleaner, until the joint is once more free of sand. John sees how polished and gleaming, how malleable and smooth the joint surfaces have become.

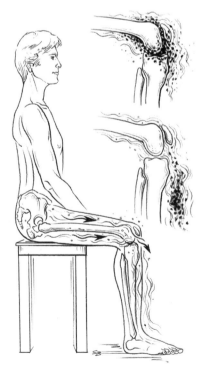

23. Purifying the knee

After this exchange, John feels immediate relief in the knees. The problem has not disappeared entirely, but through daily dialogue with the knee (with variations in the pictorial language), the problem slowly vanishes and the knee returns to health.

Negative Thinking and Joint Problems

Is there a connection between thought, imagery and joints? Absolutely. But not as directly as you might think. Our joints will not seize up the instant we think harmful thoughts. If this were the case, we could hardly think of anything negative without the body reacting to it immediately. We would have permanent stress from the very act of having to think only of the positive. Fortunately, the body has a dependable resistance to negative situations. But if we follow a pessimistic model of thinking over many years, this can express itself sooner or later in physical symptoms.

Are negative thinking and arthritis related? Could arthritis be the result of constant nagging criticism? Does inflammation arise from inflammatory thinking? Would our joints be healthier if we stopped criticizing ourselves and other people (a natural connection)?

A person who exists in the purely physical-material world cannot be expected to agree with these reflections. There are, however, many despairing people who, despite medical intervention of various sorts, continue to suffer great pain. Such individuals might try listening deeply within themselves to decide if a connection could exist between their thoughts and their physical condition.

A surprising find

Recently I heard a speech by Hans-Peter Dürr, the former director of the Max Planck Institute for Physics in Munich [from DRS 2—Perspektiven vom 27.07.2008 Wissenschaft und Weisheit. Eine Begegnung mit dem Atomphysiker (A Meeting with Nuclear Physicist) Hans-Peter Dürr].

The Max Planck Institute is one of the leading research centers in the world. What the director had to say was simply astonishing. He had spent fifty years of his life trying to find primal matter, the smallest material from which everything else is put together. His surprising finding was this: at the end of all division—the final splitting of particles—there was nothing to be found except information. Information comes before matter, he said. There is no one smallest piece of matter with certain volume and weight from which everything is put together like building blocks. Dürr says: "Mit dem Geist fängt Alles an." ("Everything starts with the mind.") *Geist* or *mind* is primal to matter. There is a relationship between information and matter, and information comes first. You and everything around you are nothing but information put into matter, says the physicist. An esoteric example, you may protest, but I must remind you that I am quoting from a premier scientific source. Indeed, the fact that the information we carry (in the form of thoughts and images) can affect our physical body becomes much more obviously resonant.

The Diversity of Bones

Without bones we would move like amoebae, that is, as a rather unappetizing mass of organs and muscle. The first short-legged animals were similar, dragging themselves on their bellies over the rough primeval terrain. Bones allowed them to lift their bodies off the ground to limit friction. Bones are the solution to gravity.

The marrow of bone is the cradle of red blood cells, and bone also serves to protect important organs like the lungs, heart, and brain. Bones store calcium and are a kind of suspension bracket for muscles, organs, and ligaments. Bones allow us to move quickly and in many directions. Bones have diversity in their form as well as in their function. Long bones (arms, legs, fingers) are mostly found in the limbs; flat bones (pelvis, shoulder blade, rib, skull) protect; short bones (carpal, tarsal), and irregular bones (facial bones, heel bone) connect.

Diving into a bone

Start by moving an arm to get a sense of its present mobility. Now focus on the lower arm. Touch the bones on the inner and outer side of the elbow. These are the ulna and the radius, the two bones of the lower arm. The bone surfaces feel smooth. This silky covering surrounding the bone is the periosteum, a membrane that is very sensitive and well supplied with blood.

Now imagine the underlying compact bones. They are not solid throughout, but tubular. This saves weight without compromising strength. The wall of the tube is called the cortex and is ninety-five percent collagen, packed especially thickly.

Cortical bone cells are constructed in layers called lamellae, organized around a central canal (the Haversian canal). The osteocytes embedded in cortical bone are not isolated, but rather exchange information through tentacle-like extensions (Illustration 21).

Diving deeper into the bone, we come to the trabeculae. This part of the bone (spongy bone) has many holes and looks like Swiss cheese. The solid 'cheese part,' trabecular bone, is aligned so that it cushions the effects of most forces it commonly encounters.

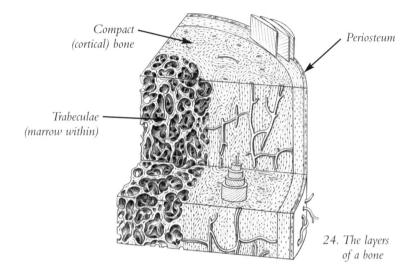

Compact
(cortical) bone

Periosteum

Trabeculae
(marrow within)

24. The layers
of a bone

The 'holes' in bone reduce its weight. Together, all the bones in our body weigh only fifteen or sixteen pounds (seven kilograms). Yet, depending on the size and type, bones are capable of supporting over 1,300 pounds (600 kilograms), as in the case of the thighbone (femur). For this we can thank in part the alignment of the trabeculae. Trabeculae (meaning 'small beams') can be likened to the steel struts of a crane or to the Eiffel Tower.

Move the arm now with awareness of its multiple layers; it feels buoyant. A distinct respect has been gained for this complex entity that is light, strong, and in a state of constant renewal.

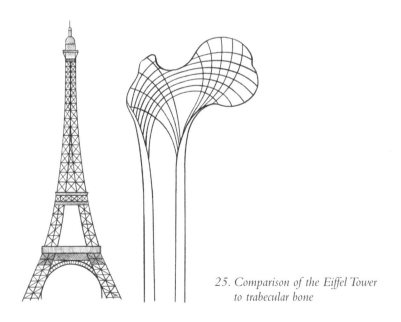

25. Comparison of the Eiffel Tower
to trabecular bone

In the middle of the bone we encounter the marrow. Red marrow contains stem cells for the immune system and for the production of blood. Yellow marrow is made of fat; as we age it increases in proportion to red marrow. In adults, red marrow is found, above all, in the ends of long bones, in flat bones, and in the vertebrae. The shafts of long bones hold yellow marrow. Chinese health practitioners recommend imagery and breathing exercises to build red blood-producing marrow. This rejuvenates the body and makes it more resistant. By projecting thought into bone marrow we can achieve flowing and active sensations.

We have seen (in the earlier example of increased blood flow to cartilage in the hip joint) that being in contact with red bone marrow is helpful for nourishing the joints. This process also helps to strengthen the immune system and shorten recovery time in the case of illness.

Strengthening the red bone marrow

Imagine the power of your thoughts causing the red bone marrow to be more active and dynamic. The marrow surges with activity, our inner Fountain of Youth.

For people with more intense dispositions, the marrow can also be likened to a glow that is strengthened by gentle breezes. Send the breath into the marrow and imagine

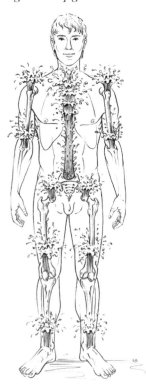

26. Bone marrow as a Fountain of Youth

the stem cells becoming stronger and more active. The flared wings of the pelvic bones are sites for a rich source of marrow. Try to visualize this. If you are not immediately successful, do not be put off. Allow time for your perception to develop; by taking time you will arrive sooner at your objective.

Also picture the marrow in the vertebral bodies of your spine. It strengthens the back and the entire immune system. Visualize marrow within the breastbone and in the head of the femur, the part of the thighbone that forms the hip joint. Send energy from your breath into the red marrow that is present throughout the entire body, aware that the immune system renews itself each minute.

Osteoporosis

In osteoporosis, the bones slowly de-mineralize. They become hollow and in consequence brittle. Attempts are often made to correct this condition by consuming calcium; the question is whether the calcium actually reaches the bone. An interesting discovery was made that in certain nations where milk was not consumed, osteoporosis was hardly present. In a report in 2005, twenty-seven studies of calcium supply and bone strength were compared and it was determined that there was little relation between the consumed amount of calcium from milk and bone strength. Calcium intake is important, but the composition of nutrients seems more important than the actual amount of calcium taken in. In the selected cultures, there was also much agricultural work, where the bones were loaded—in opposition to office work. In certain cultures dance is also integral, both at work and at festivals. Dancing is an all-round form of exercise that stimulates the body to build bone tissue. If the dancing is also joyful, this too must certainly play a role—in contrast to an exercise program that is yet another duty to fulfill. Physical inactivity is what most promotes osteoporosis. Once again, attitude is the deciding factor.

The bones as lodestones

Imagine that the bones are magnets able to draw to themselves all nutrients required for building bone tissue (calcium, vitamins, minerals). They draw nutrients to the periosteum, to the bone cortex, to the trabeculae, and finally to the marrow. They attract nourishment to the joint.

Standing, bounce a little with lightly bent knees. Imagine how, as a result, the bone cells become activated to build new tissue. The bones become full and strong, robust and resilient.

Whenever you are walking, imagine that every step strengthens the bones. The bones love to bear weight; it makes them hardy, flexible, and untiring.

Chapter 5: The Muscles

Tense muscles accelerate aging. If muscles are thin and short, they inhibit blood flow. Joints are compromised, the skin becomes wrinkled, and you don't feel well. Massage and hot baths are helpful, but imagery can work instantly.

Flexibility as an Everyday Activity

Where does movement originate? It comes from your mind. If the body is well coordinated, we are in command of optimal mobility. Coordination is a function of the brain; the brain is the site of movement control and of the image you have of your own posture and movement. Mobility is improved through clear images of how to coordinate and move the body.

Naturally some people are more flexible than others; the goal is not to become a contortionist, but for each individual to enjoy a lifetime of healthy flexibility appropriate for him or herself.

Muscle stretching is the most familiar method of increasing flexibility. Benefits include sensing a muscle's condition, helping it to relax, and (usually) temporarily lengthening it.

Stretching has its due place in fitness training, but as long as posture and habitual ways of moving are inefficient, it is not the most lasting method to improve muscle length and pliancy. Poor posture commandeers the muscles that correct our balance when there is instability. These muscles are thus overworked and as a result are tense and unavailable for the task of movement. As soon as posture improves, the muscles begin to relax and become more flexible. A classic example is the shoulder blade, which many people carry too high on the body. Perhaps this is a kind of protective response, in which we use this relatively flat bone as a shield to ward off life's onslaughts. In any case, we are better off when the shoulder blades are not always trying to whisper in the ears, but rest quietly on the rib cage.

Our goal is a youthful attitude, because this is what keeps us young. In the language of movement, this means that our daily life should be flexible and mobile. The opposite image would be constant tension throughout the day—with massage and stretching courses every other evening to compensate. Healthy habits keep us young, so we make healthy movement a constant habit!

So how do you accomplish this? You can use imagery tools mentioned at the beginning of this book, anatomical and metaphorical images of joint function and you can work directly with the muscles. Said simply, if we succeed in perceiving length in our muscles, we actually become used to long muscles, because what we sense can be stored in the brain as a new code for flexibility. Achieving flexibility is thus a matter of noting sensation.

The muscles are listening

Raise and lower your arm. Now say aloud, "My muscles are cramped and tense." Raise and lower the arm again and say, "My muscles are elastic and mobile." Compare the feeling in the first attempt with the feeling of the second. Flexibility follows our thoughts. (See Motivation and Rejuvenation, page 10.) An example of this is presented in the following exercise.

The rhomboid muscle as chewing gum

This exercise will lengthen the muscles between the shoulder blades. The muscles we are interested in are the rhomboids located between the inner border of the scapula and the spinous processes of the thoracic spine. The shoulder blade might be imagined as a holster that is placed on a belt of muscle running from the rib cage to the vertebral column. This belt is composed of the rhomboid and the serratus anterior muscles. The belt should be flexible. If the shoulders are accustomed to being carried high up, the rhomboid muscles are tight.

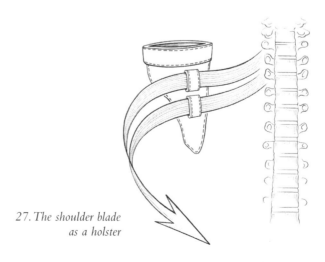

*27. The shoulder blade
   as a holster*

Curl the fingers of both hands against each other as shown in Illustration 28. With the arms horizontally in front, curve your spine forward, while at the same time extending your arms. This movement lengthens the rhomboid muscles so that you get a good feel of them between your shoulder blades.

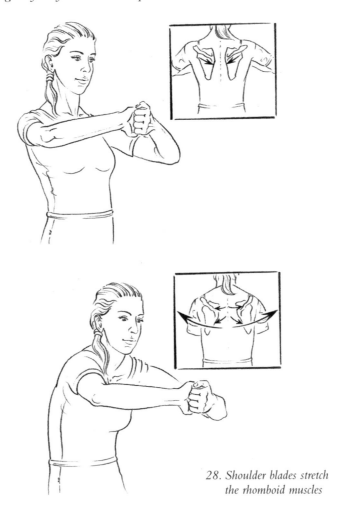

28. Shoulder blades stretch
the rhomboid muscles

After performing this movement three times, you can imagine the shoulder blades hanging from the spinous processes of the vertebral column via the rhomboid muscles. When something hangs, it pulls the structure on which it hangs lengthwise. Allow the weight of the shoulder blades to stretch the rhomboid muscles like chewing gum. The medial borders (the long sides parallel to the spine) of the shoulder blades slide downward and stretch the muscles. Visualize the elongated muscle and experience it in this lengthened state. The shoulder blades are positioned so that their good posture will naturally stretch the rhomboid muscles.

Muscles—The Desire to Move

Children and in fact all young animals and those young at heart have a strong urge to move. Muscles are the answer to this desire, and movement is the elixir of all creatures. Almost all animals have muscles, even a very simple and tiny animal like the hydra commonly found in ponds. Only single-celled organisms can manage without muscles; they move with the help of small extensions called *cilia* and by quickly changing the shape of their bodies. As living beings evolved and their size increased, this method became impractical. A strong frame developed, the skeleton, to which muscles could be attached. Muscles are thus a very early evolutionary experiment, and within our bodies we carry the same building blocks of muscle construction as very simple living organisms.

Muscle is the most abundant tissue. Many fish are up to sixty percent muscle, while antelopes and humans are from forty to fifty percent; the dolphin is an adorable torpedo of muscle.

If our muscles are fit, we have assisted the largest system in the body to reach a healthy condition. In humans, muscles have three classifications: those that move the skeleton (striated muscle), heart (cardiac) muscle, and muscles that are responsible for organ function (smooth muscle). Skeletal muscle produces movement, maintains posture and alignment, and generates body warmth. Cardiac muscle pushes blood through the heart chambers. Smooth muscle, among other functions, enables childbirth, digestion, and emptying the bladder. The interior structure of skeletal muscle is very regular. Smooth muscle, on the other hand, is less regular in its organization. Cardiac muscle has qualities of both.

Muscles have cells of different lengths. A muscle cell is also known as a muscle fiber. In some muscles the fibers run along the entire length of the muscle and can be many inches long. This is possible because during evolution many single muscle cells fused into one large cell, and this explains why these particular muscle cells have many nuclei, but are unable to divide. If injured, reserve cells will be installed—waiting in the background, so to speak, for their grand entrance.

Within the muscle cell, and arranged with geometric precision, are two bands of protein. Made up of either thick or thin filaments, the bands are each arranged in their own compartments within an area called the *sarcomere*. In the diagram we can see the dark myosin filaments with the lighter actin filaments between them.

When a muscle contracts, these filaments slide into each other. They slide apart again when the muscle stretches. Depending on the way you look at it, you could say that the actin draws the myosin to it or that the myosin skims over the actin.

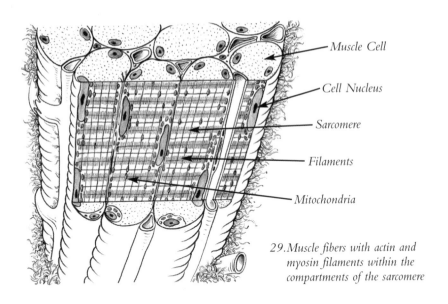

Muscle Cell

Cell Nucleus

Sarcomere

Filaments

Mitochondria

29. *Muscle fibers with actin and myosin filaments within the compartments of the sarcomere*

30. *Muscle filaments sliding away from each other (above) and toward each other (below)*

Muscle lengthening

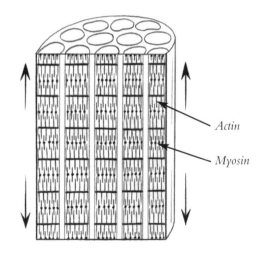

Actin

Myosin

Muscle shortening

Sarcomere

The power stroke in muscle

Actin and myosin filaments are not simply bars or wands. The myosin filaments have heads attached to their ends that perform a dance. These filaments nod their heads, as it were, and push forward or backward against the actin filaments. Then they release the actin filaments in order to nod their heads again. This nodding is called the 'power stroke.'

When a person dies, the myosin heads remain attached to the actin, because they lack the energy (the ATP) to uncouple themselves. This is called rigor mortis.

The cable pull of the filaments

The following image helps to better understand the three phases of myosin movement. If we want to pull a cable toward us, we must grip it, then pull it toward us and let go, in order to grip it at a place further along. Our two hands work alternatively one after the other, to keep the movement ongoing. Myosin has six 'hands' and accomplishes this with admirable smoothness.

We can describe the three different phases thus:

1. the instant of gripping the cable (the myosin heads come into contact with actin);
2. the instant of pushing or sliding (when we pull the cable toward us and the actin glides past the myosin), and;
3. the instant of release (the myosin lets go of the actin).

Because myosin sits in the middle of strands of actin, it is as though we were pulling cables to us from each side—and for this we would need the six arms that the myosin actually possesses.

The filaments as a rowboat

The image of a rowboat is another way to understand the lengthening and shortening aspect of muscle cells. Here the myosin is the boat, the myosin heads are the oars, and the actin is the water. The power stroke is the movement of the oars in the water. This image illustrates the fluid feel of muscular action.

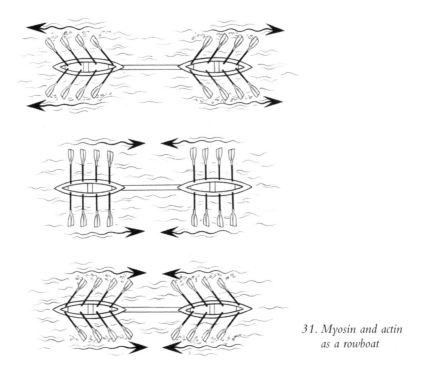

31. Myosin and actin
as a rowboat

The contraction of organs

Organ (smooth) muscle cells can also shorten. These movements are necessary, for instance, during digestion (*peristalsis*) or when emptying the urinary
bladder.

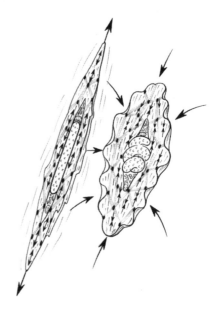

32. Contraction of an
organ muscle cell

The filaments in organ muscle cells are not arranged in the same manner as in skeletal and cardiac muscle cells. When organ muscle cells contract, they change from a long shape into an oval ball. In fact, the cell nuclei twist, which saves space.

Gliding muscle filaments

Let us apply this new image of muscles to the deltoid muscle. This muscle is attached on the upper arm and the outside of the shoulder. It assists in lifting the arm.

Place the right hand on the left deltoid muscle. Lift the left arm and imagine the muscle filaments beneath the right hand sliding past each other. Repeat the movement seven times, with the same image. Now lift both arms together and compare the ease of the movement. Notice that the arm you moved previously feels lighter and more mobile. Repeat the exercise on the other side.

Strength through sensing the body

Sitting down, hold a one-pound weight or a book in your right hand. Lift the weight to the front, concentrating on the performance of the arm muscles. Put down the weight or the book and concentrate. Sense the entire body from the head to the feet, including the chair surface and the floor under the feet. Retain the sense of the entire body when you now pick up the weight or the book. Notice that it is now easier to lift the weight or book. When strength training, being conscious of your entire body makes tension-free training possible.

Exercising with Savvy

For the best results keep the following points in mind:

- If we exercise with tension and poor posture, we will be *tenser* afterward and will have reinforced our poor posture as well. It is always important to train with concentration and imagery, thereby encouraging good posture and balanced muscle tone.

- It is best to begin with simple exercises. Start slowly and reserve time at the end to cool down.

- When using weights or an elastic band, they should provide resistance appropriate to the individual. Unchallenging training is not useful; training that is too intense promotes strain. The exercises should involve exertion, but should under no circumstances cause pain.

*Note: elastic bands for exercise come in different widths, lengths and elasticity and are available at most sporting-goods stores. The best –known brand is Thera-Band®. See *Resources* in the Appendix section at the back of this book.

- Excessive speed when performing exercises limits strength building. Above all, muscles should be lengthened slowly.

- Exercise should be varied. Be ready to try something new rather than practicing the same exercises repeatedly. Having fun is more important than dogged repetition.

- Balance is the basis of coordination; reinforce this concept every day. Unfasten yourself from the weight machine and occasionally train with free weights, on a ball, on one leg, and so on. (More on this below).

- Keep your eye on the goal of the exercise. Knowing why you are doing something leads more quickly to the objective. Imagine a slim, taut belly while doing abdominal exercises.

- Support your exercise with an inner dialogue: "My muscles will be strong and flexible. My spine is long and mobile." The result: the benefits of training are doubled.

- Exercise every part of the body, even when your primary goal is only to have a slim midriff. The back, shoulders, and legs also need training.

- Alternate between strength training and exercise that works the lungs and circulatory system (endurance). Exercise two to three times a week for strength and two to three times a week for the circulatory system.

- Exercise for the circulatory system should be varied and not exhausting. Exhaustion weakens the immune system. Swimming, hiking, cycling, brisk walking: practiced in moderation, they all rejuvenate.

- Even twenty minutes of strength training two to three times a week is beneficial. It doesn't have to be an exotic method, performed on the latest state-of-the-art exercise machine. It is crucial that the mind is involved. Push-ups, pull-ups, and good old abdominal crunches, practiced mindfully, bring greater results than the latest fitness trend practiced without care or perception.

- Leave adequate time to recover. If, after exercising, you move directly to a stressful situation, the benefits of training will be lost. Recovery is part of training.

- Breathing allows energy to flow through the body and promotes release while exercising. Therefore, use good breathing practices when exercising.

- Having fun encourages endorphin production. So enjoy your exercise and make use of appropriate images and self-conversation to keep up your good mood.

Imagery for Toned Abdominals

A slim taut abdomen and a strong back are not just aesthetically pleasing, but a sign of fitness, meaning well-trained muscles that adequately support and stabilize our joints. An unfit and awkward appearance does not exactly raise self-esteem. It is worthwhile for everyone, including those who are by no means 'fitness freaks,' to have toned muscles. Such a person has more energy and stamina, a better disposition, more motivation, and avoids injury.

Unlike the usual methods for abdominal muscle training, we have a decisive advantage. Our use of imagery and concentration increases the positive outcome of every exercise many times over.

Exercise for the back and abdominal muscles should, however, be enjoyed with care. Begin slowly and each week build in small increments. This is the golden rule and the best way to gain strength. And as we practice the exercises, the more we concentrate on the gliding of muscle filaments, instead of simply straining the muscles, the more we create an elegant figure.

Vertical and horizontal abdominal muscles

The vertical abdominal muscle, the *rectus abdominus*, is the site of that most desired of attributes, the 'washboard' or 'sixpack' stomach. The transverse abdominal muscle (*transversus abdominus*) is particularly important for the health of your back. In the following exercise (traditional in form, but performed with new perception), you will alternate your awareness between the rectus abdominus and the transversus abdominus muscles, ultimately creating better protection for the back and a slimmer waistline.

Gliding abdominals

Lie on the ground, your fingers laced behind your head. This protects the neck from strain, as during the exercise it should stay as relaxed as possible.

When lifting the head, shoulders, and upper body, concentrate on the internal gliding-together of the rectus abdominus muscle. The top of the sternum reaches toward the pelvis as the alternating muscle filaments slide together. At all times, the neck harmonizes with the lengthening torso.

When lowering the upper body, concentrate on the gliding together of the filaments in the transverse abdominal muscle. The waistline will be slimmer as a result. This sliding of the filaments is what creates a 'wasp waist.'

Repeat the exercise slowly and mindfully, eight times only. Use images—a cable, a boat, or a simple anatomical picture—that will help develop a sense of gliding within the muscle.

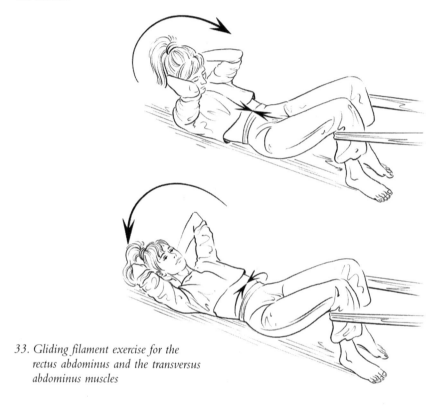

33. *Gliding filament exercise for the rectus abdominus and the transversus abdominus muscles*

The following exercise tones the abdominal and thigh muscles, and relieves pressure on the back:

Leg lifts for the hip flexor and abdominal muscles

Lying on your back with your arms relaxed on the floor next to your torso, lift your feet, one after the other, from the floor so that your knee aims for the chest. The back remains on the floor. The knees do not straighten, but stay relaxed.

Visualize the transverse abdominal muscle and sense how it holds the lower back in its supportive grip. Repeat the movement 20 times, moving loosely and breathing rhythmically with the movement of your legs. Return your feet to the floor and note that your back will feel expansive and more relaxed.

You can increase your strength each week by doing 4 extra leg lifts, until several weeks later you have reached about 50 repeats.

34. *Alternating leg exercise for hip flexor and abdominal muscles*

The following is a specialized exercise for the rectus abdominus muscle that will also help to straighten and lengthen the spine. Use a wide elastic strip made of rubber (see Appendix for a reference for Thera-Band®). I recommend a mid-strength band. (If using a Thera-Band® it will be green or blue.)

Sit and get strong

Sit on a chair with your back to the band attachment site, as shown in Illustration 35. Hold the ends of the band, slide the band over your shoulders and press your arms against the sides of your rib cage. The band should be tight enough that you are able to pull against it with the abdominal muscles. Now curve the spine forward. In order for the flexing of the spine to take place along the whole length of the spine, tilt the pelvis backward (the upper part moves to the back), and curve the head downward. Once you have arrived in a fully curved position within your comfort range, slowly straighten the spine back up. Do this slowly and with control while imagining the abdominal muscle filaments sliding away from each other. Stop when your back is straight and do not arch your back. Imagine the filaments sliding together as the back curves forward again. Then see the abdominal muscle filaments sliding apart once more as the back straightens. Repeat the exercise eight times while being fully aware of the action of the muscles.

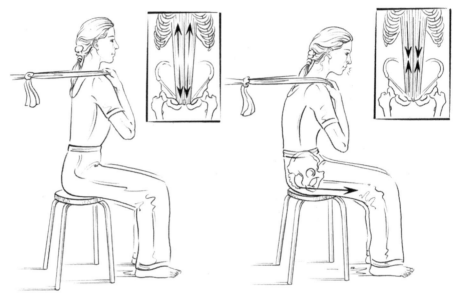

35. Chair exercise for the rectus abdominus muscle

The following is an excellent way to strengthen the abdominal oblique muscles. At the same time the exercise improves your posture when sitting, and strengthens and stretches the spinal rotators (*multifidi, rotatores, and semispinalis* muscles).

Sit and turn for strength

Fasten the Thera-Band® behind you. Sitting on a stool and holding the ends of the band, rotate the torso to the right and left, with alternate arms extending. Breathe deeply. Hold the band firmly in both hands, elbows close to your rib cage. Turn the upper body to the right and then to the left, pulling the band to the front while turning. The upper body should be tilted forward a little. Take care to initiate and perform the movement as much as possible with the upper body.

When turning to the right, visualize how the left external oblique and the right internal oblique muscles slide together. When turning to the left, visualize how the

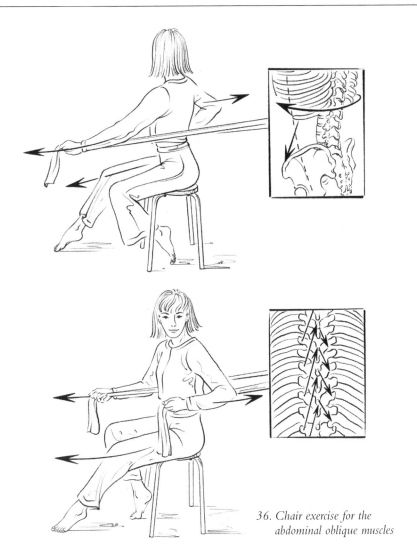

36. Chair exercise for the abdominal oblique muscles

right external oblique and the left internal oblique muscles slide together. The deep muscles of the back also help to perform this rotation of the torso. Repeat the turning movements 10 times, every week adding 2 repetitions until 30 repetitions are reached.

While strength training, we think mostly about the muscles. But the organs are also moved and exercised. If you concentrate on the organs, you will be astonished to discover that the exercises are easier to do and that the abdomen becomes firm more rapidly. Why is this? Inadequate tonicity in the organs often causes the abdomen to protrude, despite exercising the muscles. As we shall see in the chapter on organs, the greater part of an organ is muscle, muscle that responds to training.

Using organs like muscles

With the well-known 'crunch' exercise, that is, in the lifting of the shoulders and head while lying supine (knees bent), we can imagine that the organs take part in the movement, are even key to it. In lifting, the inner organs contract like an extra muscle; in returning they release like an extra muscle. Don't forget that working slowly doubles the result of this exercise. I recommend between 8 and 12 slow repetitions. Count to 3 for coming up, and to 6 for going down.

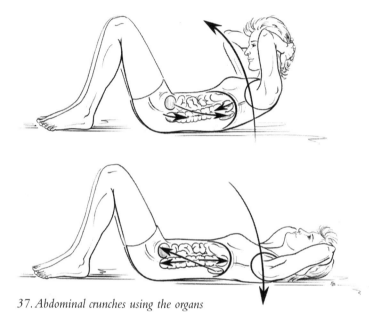

37. Abdominal crunches using the organs

Flexible Back, Elegant Arms

Before we begin to work with the back and arms, here are a few words of advice to those with back pain. There are many reasons for the current epidemic of back problems. One of them is certainly negative thinking about the back. As previously mentioned, discerning images regarding goals for a healthy back are very few. If you currently have pain, I recommend that you read *Dynamic Alignment Through Imagery,* or simply 'let go' of the pain in your life.

Pain floats away

Imagine that spasms or pain in your back are just uninvited guests that we can actively un-invite. Imagine you are spooning the back pain into small balloons waiting

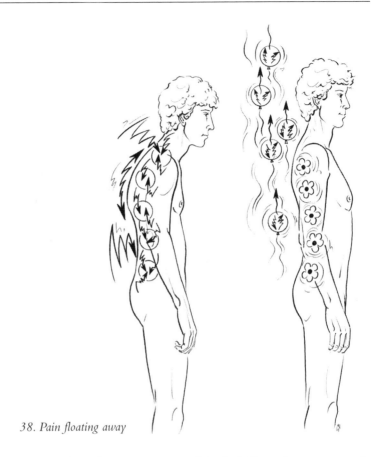

38. Pain floating away

to be released. Then watch as the pain now trapped in the balloons floats away until it can hardly be seen. A feeling of well-being—like the scent of flowers—remains.

Our training for the back begins with small movements for the rib cage. A flexible rib cage is advantageous for the back.

Flexible rib cage and back

Wrap an elastic band around your back, holding the ends in front. Move your back slowly to the right and left against the resistance of the band. Your breathing should be easy and relaxed. Imagine that the small muscles between the ribs are flexible, and that they glide smoothly. After 10 repetitions release the band. Note that your back should feel looser and your breathing freer.

Swimming on land

In this exercise you will train your back with swimming-like movements. The arms move as in breaststroke—they sweep forward and out to the sides, and then are pulled

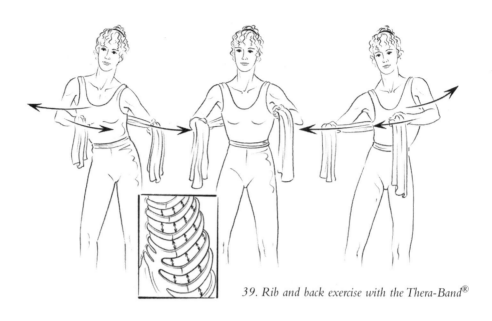

39. Rib and back exercise with the Thera-Band®

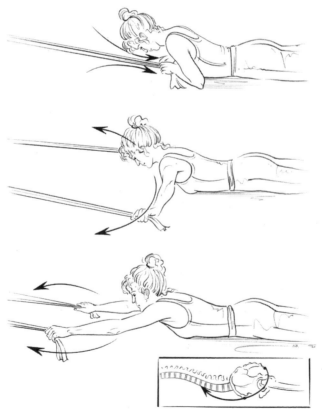

40. Reverse swimming

back in. In the final phase, the upper body is lifted slowly from the floor. The tailbone and the pelvic floor muscles actively lengthen the lower back. (Illustration 40)

The movement should then be done in the reverse direction, thus a swimming stroke in reverse. The exercise should be repeated 8 times.

After a month of sessions 3 times weekly, an elastic band can be introduced to increase the effects of the exercise. The band is passed around a strong post in front of you; the ends are held firmly in both hands. (If there is no stable support handy, a partner can help.)

Perform the reverse swimming stroke with the band 8 times.

Boxing with weights

In this exercise you will use different images to simultaneously develop flexibility, strength, and fluidity in movement. Hold two books or weights (2.5 to 5 pounds each), in either hand. Extend the arms one after the other to the front.

To increase endurance and coordination, imagine the following: the arms are supported from below as if they were a chain of floats or buoys moving through the water. Now push the arms freely forward and back in the water. You can even imagine that each single muscle cell is a small buoy floating in the water. Suspended, they are simply pushed forward and back. With this feeling, the exercise is easier; we can do it for twice as long and yet remain flexible.

41. The arms like buoys floating in water

Sitting For Health

Certain actions in life are unavoidable; they will take place anyway. So why not make the best of them and turn them into health-giving activities? They include thinking, sleeping, breathing, and, for many, also a lot of sitting. The objective for sitting is the same as for exercise in general: our posture while seated should be healthy for our joints, muscles and organs. It should be flexible and balanced. Your sitting posture expresses your mood and can look quite attractive if done well.

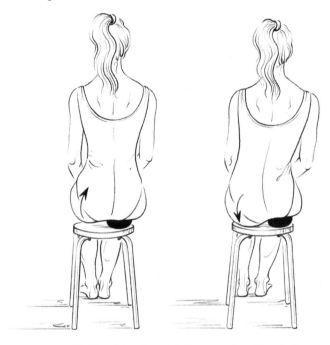

42. Exercising the pelvic floor muscles with a ball

Flexible pelvic floor

Sitting on a chair, place a Franklin Ball or Mini Roller (see Resources at the back of this book) or a rolled towel under the right side of your buttock (just in front of the right sitting bone). Now raise the left side up a little. This is exactly the challenge we are looking for! Let the left side sink slowly back onto the chair and then slowly lift it once more. This is a balancing exercise that stretches and works the muscles of the pelvic floor, abdomen, and lower back. Breathe out when the pelvis lowers and in when it lifts. Repeat the movement 7 times and remove the ball. Relax and notice that the right side of the body will feel more released, particularly the shoulder.

Now place the ball under the left buttock and repeat the exercise on the other side.

Desk workout

You can do this exercise 3 times a day while at work, without anyone noticing, because it is performed behind your desk. The exercise promotes circulation in the legs, toned muscles in the calf and abdomen, and good posture while seated—without ever leaving the Internet.

Place a Franklin Ball or rolled towel between your thighs, just above the knees. Now slightly lift and lower your legs alternatively, left and then right. The movement should be performed slowly. Notice that you are sitting more upright and that your abdominal muscles are working. Repeat the movement 20 times, breathing easily. For best results, do it 3 times a day. You (and others) will be astonished at your elegant posture at the end of the day.

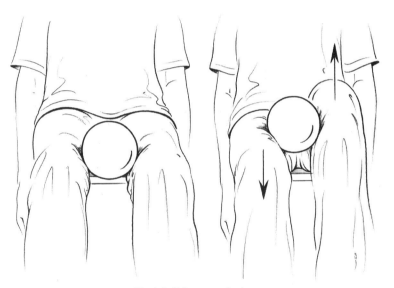

43. A ball between the knees

Releasing tension spots

A workout is not complete if we do not take time to relax. Lie comfortably on the floor, with bent knees and easy breathing.

Scan the body for areas of tension. If you feel wonderful, so much the better. If you find tension, that spot may feel like a block of wood. Imagine this mass transforming through relaxation. Notice how all stiffness fades from your muscles and how things begin to flow. A soft cloud-like feeling arises, like steam in a sauna. You can use images of soft movement as well as any of your own intuitive pictures to help stiffness melt away and woodenness turn into a calm sense of well-being.

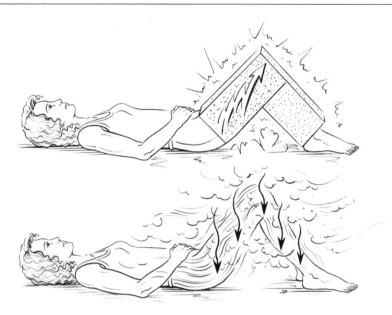

44. How to loosen a block…like a block of tension dissolving in clouds

Connective Tissue—the Elastic Envelope

Muscles require a sizable amount of structural support from connective tissue. This tissue is arranged in layers and penetrates right to the core of the muscle, where it surrounds and separates muscle filaments. Connective tissue protects the muscle from impact, and without it the muscle would be like honey leaking out of a broken jar. When the muscle shortens as it contracts, it bulges since the muscle mass is concentrated in a smaller area. This causes the connective tissue to expand; if the connective tissue is too tight, the muscle cannot contract properly.

The same is true for muscles lengthening: if the connective tissue is tight, the muscle cannot stretch to its full length. When we stretch, it is in most instances not the muscle itself that is being stretched but the connective tissue. If we are aware of this, we can use a more effective stretching technique. Muscles that are not moved and stretched regularly produce adhesions between the different layers of connective tissue. This limits free movement and reduces blood supply.

Stretching the connective tissue

To stretch connective tissue, visualize altering the collagen network. This network can be thought of as a mesh stocking that encompasses all muscles and muscle fibers within its many layers. When you stretch, visualize spreading out this three-dimensional network. Muscle flows into the expanded area created by the connective tissue web.

Remain 1-2 minutes in the stretched position, while you imagine the expanding connective tissue network and the flow of musculature into it. Envision the collagen fibers within this flow like waves on the ocean.

Many areas in the body have a strong presence of connective tissue. This is the case in the back, where many layers of connective tissue surround the muscles and attach them to bones. The lumbodorsal fascia, found in the lower back, is an integrative center for muscles in the back, pelvis, and lower limbs. It is in contact with the latissimus dorsi, gluteus maximus, and different layers of the spinal muscles. When the lumbodorsal fascia is short and tense, the intervertebral discs and the spinal joints become compressed.

Loosening connective tissue in the back

Lie on your back with the left leg stretched out and the right leg bent, with the right foot on the floor. Hold the right knee with the left hand and pull the knee to the left side. The pelvis and the leg likewise will rotate to the left. Try to leave the shoulders, especially the right shoulder, on the floor. You will soon feel a stretch in the back. Pull the left knee only far enough to feel a stretch in the connective tissue, and then remain at that point. Imagine the connective tissue lengthening like rubber bands stretching out. Imagine the cells becoming more active thanks to the stimulation (through stretching) that helps produce more collagen fibers to accommodate the new position.

Pull the right knee further to the left and remain (for at least 1 minute) in this position until the connective tissue has adjusted. Repeat the movement, visualizing the lengthening tissue, until satisfied with your progress.

Roll onto your back, stretch out both legs and compare the two sides of your back. Repeat the connective tissue stretch on the other side.

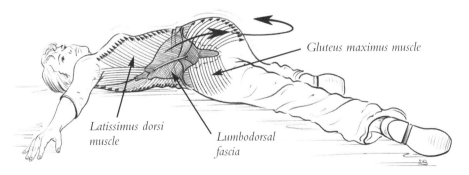

Gluteus maximus muscle

Latissimus dorsi muscle

Lumbodorsal fascia

45. Connective tissue stretch for the lumbodorsal fascia.

Fully stretching the muscles

Within the muscle, near the muscle fibers and the connective tissue, are many nerves and vessels. When a muscle lengthens or shortens these structures are naturally involved, and their arrangement normally prevents them from becoming overstretched. Vessels and nerves lie in mostly wave-shaped forms within the muscle, and are sheathed with connective tissue. If the muscle is stretched, the waves straighten out. Nerves and vessels have an intrinsic ability to extend, but not to unlimited lengths. In careless stretching, a nerve can become overstretched—a very painful experience. Care should be taken especially with the sciatic nerve, which extends diagonally down and outward from the lower lumbar vertebrae and upper sacrum, down the back of the leg.

Stretching the muscles as a whole

In the following stretching exercise we will focus our awareness on all the components of a muscle. It is important, however, that we do not stretch without warming up first; do a bit of brisk walking until you notice that your breathing has accelerated somewhat.

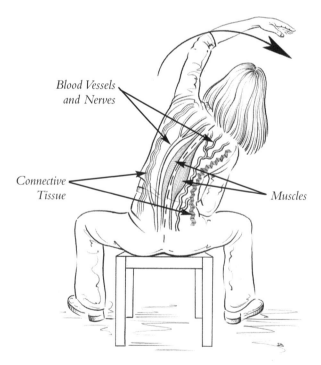

Blood Vessels
and Nerves

Connective
Tissue

Muscles

46. The stretched muscle components in symbolic form
(On the right side they are shortened, on the left lengthened.)

Sit on the floor with your legs crossed, or if that is uncomfortable, on a chair. Stretch the left arm overhead and bend the upper body to the right. The sitting bones should remain on the surface of the chair.

Imagine how the muscles, connective tissues, vessels, and nerves all lengthen: the entire muscle compartment with its ducts, sheaths, and functional support. Send your breath into the muscles, connective tissues, vessels, and nerves. Sense how they slowly lengthen.

Remain in this position for 5 deep inhalations and exhalations, then return to your starting position. To maintain the newly gained flexibility, do the stretch a second time on the same side. After 30 seconds, return to the center. The left and right sides of your body (the stretched side and the not stretched side) will probably feel somewhat different. Noting this sensation is as important as the stretch itself because, as we now know, flexibility begins in a brain with flexible awareness. What the brain has never clearly experienced can scarcely be created in movement. Stretch both arms to the front; the right may feel longer. All structures have lengthened and the cells have actively created more flexibility.

Repeat the stretch twice on the other side and sense the upper body's vertical elongation.

Chapter 6: The Organs

The inner organs play a decisive role in health and rejuvenation. Fitness and beauty, though, are generally associated with what is directly visible in outward appearance, meaning the skin and the play of muscles beneath it.

Holding onto our youthful strength is above all dependent on the efficient functioning of organs. Scarcely anyone dies of over-aged skin or weakness in the skeletal muscles. What actually defines our age is the condition of our heart, circulation, lungs, kidneys, liver, brain, and digestive tract. The organs also influence our outer appearance and behavior. A fresh-looking skin and strong muscles, for example, are only possible through the absorption of adequate proteins, carbohydrates, vitamins, minerals, and enzymes within the digestive tract. The liver and kidneys detoxify the body; the heart and vessels deliver blood to the brain, skin, and muscles. Poor circulation causes muscles to cramp; insufficient blood to the skin ages it more quickly.

The brain consumes twenty percent of our absorbed oxygen, although it makes up only one-fortieth of the body's weight. Should the heart and circulation not be working at optimal level, our cognitive and responsive functions will be weakened. According to the latest studies, our ability to respond—our reflexes—are even an indication of life expectancy.

Accordingly, over the following pages we will pay our organs a visit and with the Franklin Method® help them serve our bodies for a good while longer. The functions of the various organs will not be described in detail; further knowledge can be obtained in anatomy and physiology books. More relevant is our respect for the miraculous work of the organs and our maintenance and enhancement of their health through imagery.

Fitness for the Organs

Few of us are aware of the health of our organs—although the number of people with organ problems is enormous. An entire third of all Americans, for instance, complain of pain in one form or another, in the area of the abdominal organs. We will not deal with individual diseases—a longer book would be needed to accomplish this—but we will learn what can be achieved for the individual organs with the help of our mental powers.

Positive influences on organ health can be attained through awareness of them in ways such as the following:

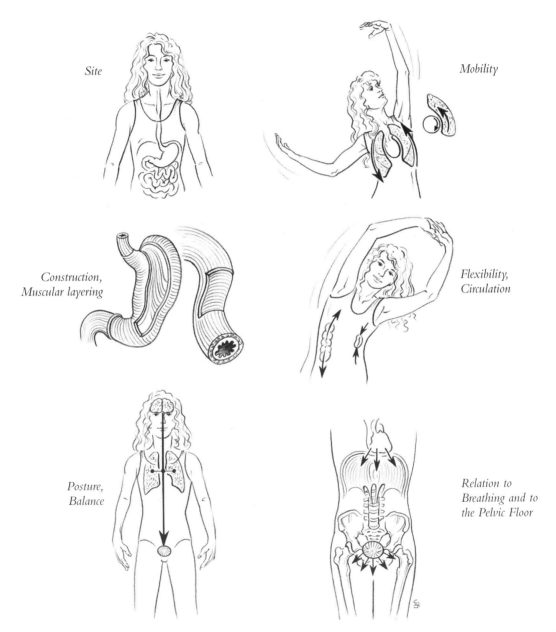

Site

Mobility

Construction, Muscular layering

Flexibility, Circulation

Posture, Balance

Relation to Breathing and to the Pelvic Floor

47. Becoming aware of the organs

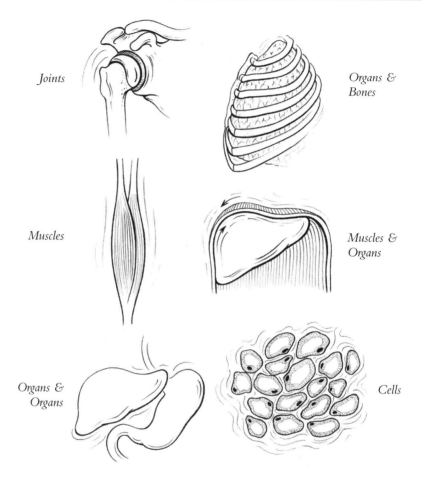

Joints

*Organs &
Bones*

Muscles

*Muscles &
Organs*

*Organs &
Organs*

Cells

48. Flexible all over

We should have at least some knowledge of the basic functions of the organs. They are *our* organs, and what can be nearer to us than our own body? We need organs more than toothbrushes, yet someone asked about the state of his or her spleen may not have even heard of it. (The spleen is an immune organ, a detoxifier, and a reservoir for blood.) But to most people, the purpose of a toothbrush is more apparent.

The organs, and not just the muscles and joints, should be an important component of our daily routine and exercise program. With this in mind, we can design movement more efficiently and effectively. As with the joints between bones, so too can movement be fostered between organs. Awareness of the joints between organs lightens the load on the muscles and promotes circulation. Whoever experiences this for the first time will be astonished at the strong influence the organs have on the body's elasticity.

The larger portion of an organ is muscle—and it requires exercise. The stomach, for example, has three layers of muscles, the intestines two. And no other muscle in the human body comes close to the muscular strength of the uterus.

The organs should have the correct tonicity, being neither too slack nor too active. This balance can be achieved with help from exercises that lengthen and shorten, stretch and unfold the organs.

Organs should remain in their original location within the body and not become compressed or pushed out of place by bad posture. Exercises for the organs can help to improve posture.

Organs work in partnership with muscles, ligaments, and other organs. The heart, for example, sits on the diaphragm and is moved about by it and even massaged (stretched and rotated: see also *Inner Focus, Outer Strength*).

As a postscript, mental awareness exercises can help to moderate the course of many illnesses.

We are flexible everywhere

In everyday life and during exercise, we will come to realize that we are flexible everywhere: in the joints, muscles, organs, and between all the elements of the body. We can imagine potential flexibility throughout the entire body. The joints are flexible, the muscles are flexible, the organs are flexible, organs next to muscles are flexible, and even cells next to each other are flexible. We will observe the positive influence this awareness has on our mental attitude.

Unrolling the organs

Sit on a chair with a level surface that allows the thighs to be horizontal when the feet are flat on the floor. Beginning with the head, bend the body slowly foreward, allowing it to hang downward and moving one segment after the other. This movement is called a 'body roll-down'; the return journey to upright is called a 'body roll-up'. Imagine that the strength in your organs helps you to perform this movement. The brain moves first, dropping forward and down, then the esophagus and larynx in the neck; the lungs bend forward, the upper abdominal organs—the liver and stomach—follow; the kidneys and the intestines next; and, to finish, the bladder.

To roll up, begin with the bladder, and then imagine the small and large intestines, followed by the upper abdominal organs (stomach, liver), the chest organs, the heart and lungs, the esophagus, and the brain. After rolling down and up, notice your pos-

*49. Training the organs
while seated*

ture. It may be that you feel more centered and upright. If performing the same movement with awareness focused on the muscles instead of the organs, your sensations will be different. Try it!

What we would like for our organs

In the first part of this book we experienced how important precise goals are for our health. As with other parts of the body, goals for the organs are usually either vague or do not exist at all. Therefore, let us take five minutes right now and write down what we might wish this year for our organs. Don't forget the principles of effective imagery: no negative images (no pain), the most vivid descriptions possible, how something feels or appears, and when a goal should be attained. In addition to typical objectives like strength, health, and well-being, motivational elements such as joy, fun, and energy should be used. For example, "This is what I would like for my kidneys: easy strength, good blood circulation, and a fun time while purifying my blood."

Saying thank you is healthy

Thanking the organs for their brilliant achievement is very beneficial to the health. The heart beats 87,000 times a day; when we breathe an average of 20,000 times, the kidneys purify the blood unceasingly; in our bone marrow 1,000,000 new blood cells develop per second. And possibly we have never said "Thank you". Initially perhaps it will take some convincing for us to say, "Thank you, liver! Good job! Keep up the good work!" and "Bravo, heart! I am in awe of your untiring accomplishments. Kidneys, you pair of beauties: thanks to you my blood is pristine!"

We naturally thank someone for a birthday present, but thanking the body, the organs, occurs to almost no one. Possibly we find it childish and naïve. The organs don't find it so—they know that saying thank you helps them.

In a study at the University of California at Davis, participants were divided into three groups. One group kept a journal of their moods, rating these daily on a scale of one to six. The second group wrote down whatever angered or stressed them; the third group wrote out all the occasions during the day for which they were thankful. The results were predictable: health and motivation improved in the thankful group. The group that fared least well was the group concentrating on anger. A classic imaginative situation: what you see before the inner eye will be carried over and heightened in your own life. So make it a daily habit to review everything good that has befallen you. Thank your bones, joints, muscles, glands, nerves and organs on a daily basis. You can begin right now!

Strengthening the organs through relaxation

As with the whole body, organs gain strength through rest. Deep relaxation allows organs to purify and regenerate themselves. The steps to reaching this relaxation are as follows:

1. *Take a comfortable position lying on a mat or bed;*

2. *Imagine an individual organ or a group of organs. To do this, visualize or sense the site, size, and form of the organ by using, if desired, an anatomy atlas or the illustrations in this book;*

3. *Be mindful of your breathing and of the gravitational pull on the organs;*

4. Create a vivid image or thought that will reach and relax this organ. In many cases, the responding sensation will be a feeling of well-being, of expansion and release in the organ.

In the following exercises we will imagine the organs in succession and with the help of self-conversation, make it possible for them to relax and regenerate.

Relaxing and regenerating the organs

Lying comfortably, say to yourself:

"My heart is calm and relaxed; peace and relaxation are in my heart. My heart is calm and relaxed; strength and renewal are in my heart.

My lungs are calm and relaxed; peace and relaxation are in my lungs. My lungs are calm and relaxed; strength and renewal are in my lungs.

My liver is calm and relaxed; peace and relaxation are in my liver. My liver is calm and relaxed; strength and renewal are in my liver.

My stomach is calm and relaxed; peace and relaxation are in my stomach. My stomach is calm and relaxed; strength and renewal are in my stomach.

My left kidney is calm and relaxed; peace and relaxation are in my left kidney. My left kidney is calm and relaxed; strength and renewal are in my left kidney.

My right kidney is calm and relaxed; peace and relaxation are in my right kidney. My right kidney is calm and relaxed; strength and renewal are in my right kidney.

My large intestine is calm and relaxed; peace and relaxation are in my large intestine. My large intestine is calm and relaxed; strength and renewal are in my large intestine.

My small intestine is calm and relaxed; peace and relaxation are in my small intestine. My small intestine is calm and relaxed; strength and renewal are in my small intestine.

(For women) My bladder and my uterus are calm and relaxed; peace and relaxation are in my bladder and uterus. My bladder and uterus are calm and relaxed; strength and renewal are in my bladder and uterus.

(For men) My bladder and prostate are calm and relaxed; peace and relaxation are in my prostate. My prostate is calm and relaxed; strength and renewal are in my prostate.

All my organs are calm and relaxed; peace and relaxation are in all my organs. Every organ is calm and relaxed; strength and renewal are in every organ."

50. Serenity on the ocean

After working with this mental exercise, take some time to get up. Roll onto your side (never get straight up from a lying position); tap your back with your free hand, and then slowly stand up.

The Heart

First the bad news: as the years roll on, the heart, like the midriff, tends to lose its svelte muscular condition. At the same time a build-up of both fat and other connective tissue is common, which can lead to reduced cardiac function. The good news is that calendar age has much less impact on heart health than was previously believed. A healthy eighty-year-old heart is quite capable of functioning as well as one forty years old. Once again, lifestyle is the key. Activities the heart loves include a brisk thirty-minute walk daily, with more strenuous pursuits three, or at most, four times a week. These might include swimming, jogging, cycling, or any activity that causes the heart to pump blood more quickly over a sustained period. (When beginning any new exercise program it is always advisable to obtain evaluation and assistance from medical professionals.)

The heart at home

The heart rests in a flexible area called the *mediastinum*, bordered by the lungs, diaphragm, spine, and uppermost rib. Nearby are the *thymus* and thyroid glands, the great vessels (large blood vessels attached to the heart), the esophagus, and the larynx, or windpipe. The heart lies at the sides and front of the lungs. We can find its position by placing the inside right wrist just to the left of the lower part of the sternum, or breastbone.

In appearance the heart is a tapered sphere, with its apex on the bottom left and base on the upper right. It is enclosed in the *pericardium*, a protective sac attaching it directly to the diaphragm. Muscular tension and shallow breathing disturb the natural action of the heart riding on the diaphragm (an avoidable problem). Ligaments connect the pericardium to the cervical spine (the neck) and to the sternum, or breastbone. Due to this relationship our posture directly influences the state of our heart.

Breathing gives the heart not only a ride up and down on the diaphragm but also a constant massage. On inhalation, the diaphragm descends, and, because the heart is suspended from above by the aorta and ligaments, it receives a gentle stretch with each breath. On exhalation, as the diaphragm relaxes and ascends, the heart is gently compressed.

Just above the heart is the thymus gland, an immune organ that in infancy and childhood is larger than the heart itself. In early life the thymus is a kind of training center for the specialized cells that will comprise the adult immune system. As these cells develop, the thymus shrinks. Interestingly, it is the thymus rather than the heart that is heart-shaped.

Unlike the parallel lengthwise arrangement of skeletal muscle fiber, cardiac muscle fiber is branched and presents an overlapping three-dimensional grid. Even the myofibrils (of end-to-end myofilaments within the sarcomere, or contracting unit) can be branched. The nuclei of skeletal muscle cells are on the outer edges; those of the heart are centrally positioned. Cardiac muscle fibers are shorter and wider; they are hardy and supplied with more numerous mitochondria and abundant sarcoplasm. Optimizing contraction where most needed, heart muscle is wrapped around the ventricular openings.

Some cardiac cells are capable of endocrine function and the heart has its own conduction system. Special pacemaker cells regulate the heartbeat to approximately seventy beats per minute. The nervous system outside the heart influences, but neither initiates nor controls, the heartbeat. In this sense the heart functions independently. Hormones produced within the heart regulate blood pressure and electrolyte balance.

The following is a popular workshop exercise for posture and motivation. Motivation and heart health are close relatives. In a ten-year study of 1,300 participants, it was established that those with a positive outlook on life were at under half the risk of heart disease as those without. This reduction was the equivalent to the difference between smoking and not smoking. So here's to affirmative inner voices and the imagination!

A lifted heart is a healthy heart

We'll begin with a short experiment. Let the upper body slump. This influences both the heart and our mood. Straighten up again, place your palm over your heart and picture it in your mind. Breathe deeply into the heart and imagine it floating easily like a small balloon or as if suspended by a cloud. Repeat inwardly 3–6 times, "A lifted heart is a healthy heart." Then breathe deeply into the heart 3 more times and say inwardly, "I breathe gladness into my heart; I breathe ease and relaxation into my heart."

*51. Hand on the heart—heart in the clouds.
The heart supported by soft clouds*

Remove your hand and observe how you feel. How does it feel now to slump? It may be that slumping has become counter-intuitive and that maintaining good heart posture feels natural.

Heart on a swing

Picture the diaphragm moving the heart and lungs up and down with every breath. This rhythmic movement relaxes the heart and lungs, and increases blood flow. The heart and lungs are constantly rocked, like a baby being calmed.

Now take a short walk and observe how the small impact of each step gently agitates and loosens the heart and lungs. The heart loves this movement; it is gently shaken and receives more blood. Say to yourself, "My heart relaxes with the rocking of my diaphragm; my heart is cradled and protected."

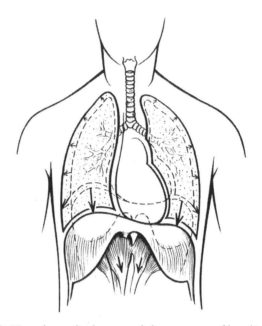

52. Heart, lungs, diaphragm, and the movement of breathing

Preventing arteriosclerosis

A look at *arteriosclerosis* reveals that the image of blood vessels calcifying like old pipes is actually, under certain circumstances, not far off. The newest research indicates that heart attacks may be attributed to an inflammatory response. But blood vessels cannot be compared to metal pipes; they are layered and considerably more flexible. Excess LDL (low density lipoprotein, the 'bad' cholesterol), does not simply hang around in a vessel; it adheres to and damages the vessel walls. Injury produces a 'call for help' inflammatory response; *macrophages* (white blood cells evolved to remove debris) and other cells soon collect in large numbers at the site of the injury, in this case the LDL deposits. The macrophages produce an accumulation of fatty cells that in turn produce a growing collagen-covered bulge. Other inflammatory-attracted molecules arrive and bring the weak collagen-coated bulge to bursting point. The lump breaks open and its contents spill out. Clotting causes a massive further build-up of cells; the artery becomes blocked and *myocardial infarction*, a heart attack, ensues.

The most important ways to prevent this process are common knowledge: exercise (strength and endurance), good nutrition, not smoking, an optimistic outlook on life, and positive body image with a regular and precise organic imagery workout. In this book we will work extensively with these last two.

Cleaning out the coronary blood vessels

Imagine the coronary arteries, the vessels supplying the heart itself, being scrubbed down by a nifty team of artery-cleaning experts. They roam through the vessels with an arsenal of special instruments, leaving behind spacious passageways and sparkling clean, smooth walls. Through these corridors blood can now flow unimpeded. Naturally you can create this cleaning militia with your own imagination; by no means does it need to resemble the illustration in this book.

This picture, like all the others showing imaginative images, is merely a suggestion and not the only way to achieve the desired effect.

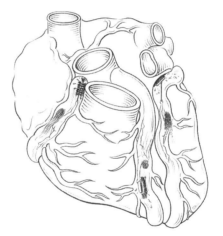

53. A cleaning team for the heart

With increasing years, residue is sometimes deposited in the tissues of the heart. Within individual cells, substances known as *lipofuscin granules* can develop. These are remnants of cellular waste material that have not been completely eliminated.

Rinsing the heart with spring water

Imagine that the heart is to be freed of all residue. The cells of the heart will be washed in spring water to clear them of these remains. We shall feel immediate relief in the heart. We shall rinse the cells with spring water until the last bits of residue have been washed away. It is useful to see the pure water, feel the water, and also hear it gushing through your cells until it flows in and out of the cells. Let us say inwardly, "My heart is free; the cells of my heart are purified and fully functional. My heart cells are motivated and well supplied with blood."

Naturally the same exercise can be applied to other organs in the body.

The flexible heart

The heart wall is composed of three layers. The inner wall (the *endocardium*) is the actual heart muscle and is the thickest layer. The middle layer is called the *myocardium* and the outer layer the *epicardium*. A sac called the *pericardium* surrounds the entire heart. The flexibility of this sac and of all the cardiac layers is crucial for the youthfulness of the heart. A tight pericardium is painful and strains the heart, which must then work harder.

The pericardial sac is mostly made of connective tissue. Between the epicardium and the pericardium is a fluid-filled space. This gap allows the heart to move and glide about uninhibited as it pulses. The heart 'floats' in the chest weightlessly, in a film of fluid.

Imagine the elasticity of the pericardium and of all the heart's layers. The heart can expand and contract without effort. It glides in the pericardium; it floats within its sheath; it feels suspended and free to move about unencumbered.

The heartbeat as ocean surf

We might compare the beating of the heart to the pounding of ocean breakers or to the strength of a geyser. Imagine the blood propelled rhythmically from the heart all the way to the body's periphery. Arterial blood (red) surges powerfully outward; returning venous blood (dark red or blue), by comparison, flows back calmly and deliberately. The farther we move from the heart, the softer the surge. You could say that the blood here burbles and flows quite comfortably. Here the blood flow is like the lapping of wavelets on the shore, but with more variation in the inward and outward stream. Water within the cells themselves is like the sea when its surface is calm and smooth.

Red blood cells pick up oxygen in the lungs and carry it to all other cells in the body's tissues. Certain organs rely on a large and steady delivery of oxygen—the brain and heart for example. In the following exercise we shall consciously visualize the red blood cells and begin a dialogue with them.

A dialogue with the red blood cells

I address my red blood cells thus: "Hello, red blood cells! Please listen!" All the blood cells stand to attention.

"I would like you to know how much I value your work. I wish for strength, pliancy, and oxygen for each and every one of you. Please keep all my tissues well supplied with oxygen. Please take particular care of my brain and heart. Always supply these organs plentifully with oxygen. Is there anything you would like from me? Is there something I can do to help improve your work even more?" I wait for an answer. If none is forthcoming as yet, I say to myself, "Good-bye for now. Have fun rushing through the vessels!"

In a sense, the heart is our emotional center, positioned (almost) in the middle of the chest. Here we experience strong positive emotions. We can use this energy to benefit the entire body.

Place a hand over the heart. Note the body's reaction to the following words spoken aloud: "Yes, love, happiness, joy, fun, laughter. Love, happiness, joy, fun, laughter, etc." Then say, "No, pain, envy, malice, hate."

Sense the vibrations of your voice under your hand; on another level, notice—and this is quite subtle—in response to positive expressions, the region of the heart lifts very slightly; it becomes lighter and more expansive. The heart is lifted, filled, and elevated; the region of the heart expands. With the negative expressions the heart sinks; it loses energy. The negative expressions may even bring pain. This should give us pause, compel us to take notice: if this exercise produces such strong effects, we would do well to cultivate respect for the impact of our spoken expression upon the heart. The habitual criticism of small talk, for example, can weigh heavily on the heart and is a very unattractive practice in itself.

Words to strengthen the heart

Place a hand over your heart and say, "Love, happiness, joy, fun, laughter." Better still, create a sequence of your own, using words with similarly positive meanings.

Incidentally, do not be afraid of hyperbole: when used with positive intent, such expressions can do us a lot of good. "My heart radiates happiness, joy, and love." These feelings spread to all the surrounding tissues. The tissues will be suffused with the positive emotions of the heart; they will be recharged and transformed. Sense the rapture of the heart penetrating neighboring organs; they too become immersed in joy. Spreading from the heart, euphoria arises in the organs and in all the tissues. And, as previously mentioned, joy, happiness, and love make us attractive, so that what we feel, we also attract. Imagery works by allowing us to experience in thought what we wish for in our lives.

The Vessels and Lymph

With advancing age, vessels can lose elasticity. The larger vessels experience thickening walls and less flexible collagen. This means that between single molecules of collagen, cross-links can arise that limit vascular flexibility. These changes do not have a direct relation to arteriosclerosis, that is, with deposits on the wall of an artery. The decline in flexibility, however, makes it more difficult for the heart to pump blood through the vessels. For many aging people, there is an accompanying rise in blood pressure. (These factors are associated with average weight gain in the general population as we get older.)

The construction of vessels

A vessel is a muscular hose with an inner and an outer membrane. The arteries that carry red oxygen-saturated blood from the heart have more musculature than the veins, which are equipped with small one-way valves to prevent the blood from flowing backward. Arteries branch into multiple vessels, becoming ever smaller until they are as fine as hair: they are known as the capillaries. Capillaries are so thin that in many cases no more than a single red blood cell can squeeze itself through them. As a result, red blood cells must be correspondingly elastic and bendable.

Oxygen passes from the bloodstream through the capillary wall into the intercellular space and moves from there to individual cells. If a cell cannot be reached directly, the oxygen travels via intercellular fluid from cell to cell (by diffusion) until the last cell is reached and can breathe. For the cells, teamwork is essential.

54. Capillaries have a natural branching structure comparable to that of a tree

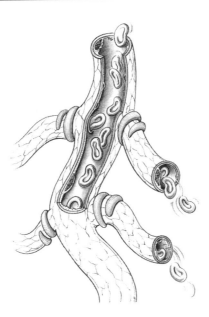

*55. Flexible red blood cells
within a capillary*

Carbon dioxide and other materials released by the cells enter the intercellular fluid in likewise manner. There it is decided which of these will be returned to the regular bloodstream and which will pursue an alternate route via lymphatic circulation. Most of those bound for the latter are cell fragments, bacteria, and viruses—substances that will be destroyed by the lymphatic system. Collectively, lymph vessels are longer than arteries and veins and, in addition, possess large and small nodes. The small nodes help lymph to transport material incrementally, as the return journey from peripheral areas is almost entirely uphill: lymphatic circulation ends at the level of the collarbone. In contrast to blood circulation, lymph flows in only one direction: from the periphery back to venous circulation.

The heart beats about once a second for our entire life. Every day it pumps a tanker-full of blood through the body—an immense accomplishment. The aging heart does not lose its basic strength in pumping; conceivably, though, it must work harder to accomplish the same task. As mentioned, when vessels lose their elasticity, the heart must work harder.

If you already have experience with imagery, you can immediately sense its positive effect on your body. Imagine that your vessels are flexible, and say inwardly, "My vessels are elastic, with plenty of room for blood." You will notice that you are able to relax your entire body instantly. On the other hand, say the opposite: "my vessels are narrow and stiff." Instantly you will feel your breath becoming slightly shallow. This unpleasant experiment is necessary in order to understand that thoughts can in fact help the vessels and, in this way, relieve the heart.

A workout for the blood vessels

Imagine the elasticity of the vessels; they stretch in different directions to facilitate the flow of blood. With every heartbeat the vessels expand to receive blood. I tell myself, "My collagen retains its flexibility for a lifetime."

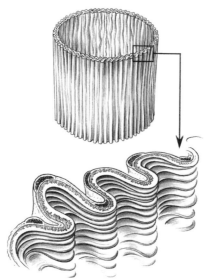

56. The stretchable, wavelike inner wall of an artery

Vessels are of an ideal construction to interact flexibly with blood. The internal structure of arteries is a wave-like cellular wall that resembles corrugated cardboard. These cells can stretch to make room for blood. Should this inner wall and the vessel itself lose elasticity, the heart must pump more strongly. Common methods to help improve the vessels include saunas and hot/cold showers. Our imagination and motivation also contribute to their health.

57. Red blood cells surfing in the bloodstream

Sensing vessel flexibility

Picture the body's vessels, miles and miles of pathways for fluid: inch-wide vessels, middle-sized vessels, and microscopic vessels allowing the passage of no more than a single red blood cell. These pathways perceive and regulate their own elasticity; they feel supple, mobile, and smooth. Sense the blood flowing unimpeded through every vessel. It is easy for the heart to pump blood; nothing stands in the way. Red blood cells tumble and slide with abandon through the vessels; they enjoy delivering oxygen while surfing gracefully through the bloodstream.

Begin to move softly, sensing the flexibility of the vessels in your movement. Visualize the capillaries, of which there are many miles in the body. It is a tight fit for the red blood cells; happily they can bend and adjust their shape to slip through the narrowest space.

Imagine the vessels actively collaborating, simplifying the work of the heart. Through body movement, the vessels are active, helping to pump blood back to the heart.

Lymph nodes and lymphatic pathways

Together with the skin, lungs, and kidneys, lymphatic circulation is one of the most important processes for detoxifying the body. We can boost this inner cleaning with the help of the following:

Movement which improves lymphatic flow and maintains the suppleness of tissue and;

Imagination which directs energy and focus to lymphatic circulation and motivates detoxification of tissue.

Spaced along the lymphatic vessels are thickened structures called lymph nodes, sites of intensive purification. The nodes are home to lymphocytes, specialized cells that destroy viruses, bacteria, and other contaminants. The pressure of intercellular fluid helps boost lymphatic flow. Lymph vessels also have small valves that inhibit backflow. The walls of the smallest vessels are in some places no wider than a single cell. These cells contain the same filaments as our musculature and are likewise able to contract. This cellular constriction helps to keep the lymph moving along. Most lymph vessels end in a fork at the left collarbone, where lymph then flows back into the bloodstream. Along the way, from the hand for instance, much has been accomplished. The fluid that found its way into lymph vessels (about ten percent of all returning fluid) has been extensively cleaned and filtered; immune cells have rendered bacteria harmless, and cell fragments have been digested by scavenger cells.

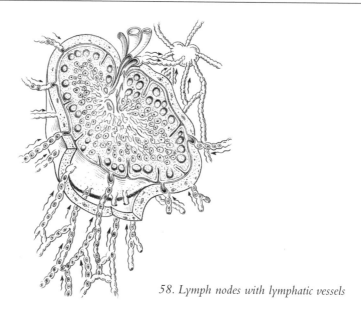

58. Lymph nodes with lymphatic vessels

Imagine the vast network of lymph vessels. Begin on the periphery of the body, at the fingers and toes. Sense the lymph being pushed (by muscles and intercellular fluid) and pulled (by the suction of the rest of the circulatory system) in the direction of the left collarbone.

Observe the veins on the inside of the left arm. They generally appear as blue stripes. If an arm is held lower than the heart, the visible veins are relatively thick. If the arm is lifted they become thin. Blood and lymph have been assisted in flowing toward the heart. Try to imagine the following:

Assisting the movement of lymph

Lymph flows toward the heart while the vessels remain in place. Stretch your left arm to the front and imagine the lymph in this arm moving toward the heart. It flows in this direction only. With your hand, stroke your arm up to the shoulder and imagine how your movement helps the lymph. Afterward compare the sensations of both arms when they are stretched out in front and lifted.

Imagine the lymph vessels and nodes efficiently cleaning the body. Thanks to lymph, the body rids itself of all that needs to be discarded. Sense how residues on the surface and in the deepest tissues are absorbed through gaps in lymphatic capillaries. As if by millions of mini-vacuum cleaners, the tissue is cleaned and readied for optimal function.

The largest portion of our blood is found in the veins, which serve as collection channels and return pathways to the heart. On occasion this leads to overload, to vein fatigue and backups in the form of varicose veins. These are more common in women, who have less strongly built veins than men.

Avoiding varicose veins

Gently tap your body all over: your legs, bottom, back, and abdomen, arms and shoulders, neck, and even your face.

Now lie on your back, with two Franklin Balls under each side of your pelvis. Stretch out both legs and lift them perpendicular to the floor. The knees do not need to be straight. This position simplifies the return flow of lymph and venous blood by allowing gravity to help. Picture blood flowing through the veins back to the heart, taking a short rest in the venous valves, and then continuing easily on its way.

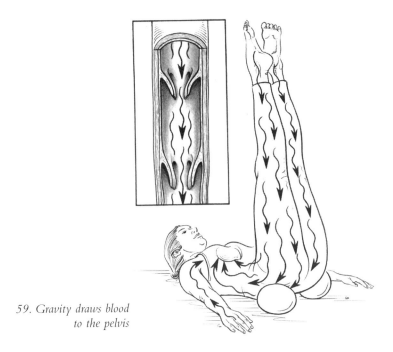

59. Gravity draws blood to the pelvis

The veins are equipped with small 'water wheels' that keep blood moving in the direction of the heart. The same image can also be applied to arterial and lymphatic flow.

Assisting the veins — helping the heart

Lie with your legs elevated. Contract your leg muscles to assist the veins with muscular movement. Imagine the venous valves becoming stronger and transporting blood to the heart with sufficient vigor. Relax your legs and shake them loose. Alternate contracting and relaxing the legs 5 times, then lower them and relax completely. The strength of the return flow relieves the heart and allows it to beat more softly.

*60. Venous cells as small
water wheels*

Stretching the blood

*Extend one arm in front of your body and imagine the millions of blood cells within
its vessels traveling toward the hand. Picture millions of red blood cells coursing in
the arteries from shoulder to hand and millions more in the veins, flowing from hand
to shoulder.*

*Imagine the simultaneous movement of these millions of cells through the vessels
from shoulder to hand and back from hand to shoulder. Experience this as an elongation, a stretching of the blood. The sensation of length in the bloodstream gives the
blood cells more ease in movement.*

TLC for the blood and vessels

Most people enjoy a little tender loving care. So do the blood and vessels.
Picture the red blood cells being caressed by the vessel walls. The red blood
cells are like soft, tiny exuberant brushes. They charge through the vessels
and the vessels send them a feeling of being loved and treasured. Likewise
the vessels adore being brushed by the blood cells. Imagine that the blood
soothes the arterial walls and hinders inflammation. The vessel walls are
strong and smooth, impervious to harm.

We can further assist the blood by imagining it swirl through the winding and meandrous pathways of the vascular system. This endows the blood with energy, like fresh spring water in a brook circling around stones and bends. The blood experiences a new interest and zest for life.

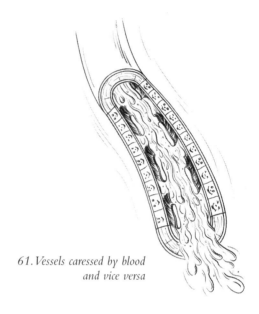

*61. Vessels caressed by blood
and vice versa*

The Lungs

The ribcage, collagen, and breathing

If your breathing is calm and the ribcage flexible, you will be able to absorb more oxygen into your body, which is a major key to healthy beauty. Infants are born with a very flexible rib cage, which facilitates breathing. For many, advancing age brings rigidity to the rib cage and weakening of both it and the respiratory muscles. I am continually shocked to discover all the people in my classes who can hardly move their ribcage any more. Subsequently, they are much less able to inhale deeply or to expel stale air on exhalation. The lungs lose elasticity owing to lack of exercise, and rigidified collagen develops, caught in the tissues. The result is inefficient delivery of oxygen to the cells. Simply expressed: "Use it or lose it".

With training, however, strength and flexibility in the rib cage and respiratory muscles can be maintained and even improved.(See chapter 5: *The Muscles*, for elastic band exercises for the rib cage.) Exercise also increases elasticity in the *pulmonary alveoli* (air sacs in the lungs where gas exchange takes place) and other lung tissue, making possible greater absorption of oxygen.

Before the blood sets off to circulate through the body, it is pumped from the heart to the lungs, to be loaded with oxygen. Oxygen is pulled into the lung tissue by respiration. Only three slim layers separate air from blood. To reach the blood, oxygen travels through the cell walls of the alveoli, through a layer of connective tissue (the basement membrane) that is fixed to the alveoli, and through the wall of the blood vessel capillaries that have carried blood to the lungs. These three layers provide a whisper-thin transition zone from air to blood.

The oxygen pathway

Begin lying down on your back. Close your eyes, observe your breath, and allow your lungs to move freely. Imagine the elasticity of the alveoli, expanding three dimensionally on inhalation to receive the air. Experience the air pouring into and then out of the lungs. Sense the abundant flow of it, the rushing stream.

Watch how the tiny delicate alveoli fill with air and how the air flows out again from the alveoli. We bid farewell to the old air and invite the new air in.

Now, just to see, do the opposite—imagine the alveoli as stiff and constricted. On inhalation the airway is now restricted.

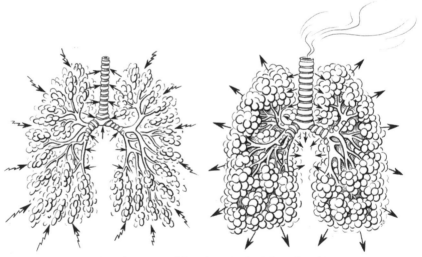

62. Left: Restricted breathing Right: Elastic breathing

Let us return immediately to positive self-talk: "My deep breathing motivates my cells to health. My alveoli are supple and elastic; my breath is free and flowing." Sense how breath suffuses the red blood cells with oxygen. The red blood cells exert a magnetic force, drawing oxygen to them through the delicate walls of the lung.

The red blood cells sound a trumpet

Oxygen might be imagined as small aqueous balls plumping up the pulmonary capillaries. The red blood cells are loaded up with these balls like small gondolas and swim happily out of the lungs, bound for the heart. We might hear a slight sound of the red blood cells bumping here and there against the vessel walls. We hear this sound from the lungs to the heart and from the heart to the whole body—through the arteries, into the smaller arteries (*arterioles*) and right into the capillaries.

63. An image from nature: the ocean spills over primeval cells

It is as if all the capillaries start singing when blood cells with fresh oxygen approach, banging against the vessel walls and singing as they come. Is this perceptible? Does such movement actually take place in the body? Blood cells fly through the small veins (venules), then the larger veins and back to the heart, to travel once more toward the lungs, where the whole game begins anew. The circulatory system, an endless river coursing through our bodies, has completed one cycle of its life-long journey.

Let us be carried along with this current. We travel through the blood vessels, ultimately to the capillaries, where we slip through small gaps (*fenestrations*) in the capillary walls, into the area that links the end of arterial blood with the origin of venous blood; into a seascape flanked by cells (the *matrix*) where intercellular fluid murmurs and undulates. Let us flow here and there among these cells. We have come to a primordial sea, our own inner ocean. We let the inner sea guide our movement, never stopping. This eternal stream, this resonant surge, spills and foams unceasingly around our cells.

The lungs and heart

Within the rib cage, near the spinal column and the heart, are the lungs. When the spine moves, they do too. If the lungs are elastic and mobile, it helps the spine, and vice versa.

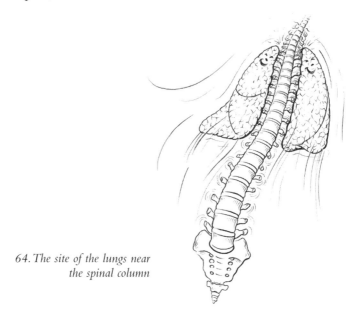

64. The site of the lungs near the spinal column

Stand up, lace your fingers together, and place them over your head. Bend your upper body sideways to the left and right, with the following image:

The heart as a ball-bearing for the lungs

The heart lies between the two lungs and acts like a ball-bearing. If we bend to the right, the left lung glides over the top of this ball, while the right glides beneath it. When bending to the left, the right lung glides along the top and the left glides beneath it. In this way the interior of the chest becomes more mobile, the rib cage expands, and cells in the lungs and heart enjoy more space to move about. Repeat the exercise to the left and right with this image. After the exercise notice the feeling of verticality in your spine and the looseness in your neck and shoulders. (Illustration 65)

If you are a more practiced imager, you can test your balance at the same time by doing the exercise standing on two Franklin Balls. This increases the effectiveness of the exercise.

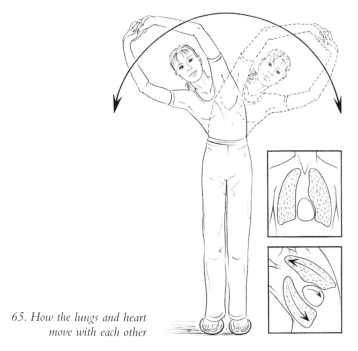

65. How the lungs and heart move with each other

Swings for the lungs

An excellent way to purify the lungs and give them energy is with 'lung swings'. This exercise de-stresses the body and calms the spirit. Place both hands on the back of your neck and visualize the lungs. Rotate your torso to the left and then to the right while breathing freely and calmly.

If this exercise hurts your back, do it very slowly and carefully and preferably while sitting. If there is no discomfort, you can rotate more quickly and to a greater degree.

Breath is very important for the effectiveness of movement. Preferably breathe through the nose and try to inhale during 2 sets of rotations to left and right, and exhale during the next 2 to the left and right. Eventually you can slow down your breathing to one inhalation/exhalation during 3 and even 4 sets.

Continue this exercise for 1–2 minutes, while imagining the lung cells suspended in their rotational to-and-fro pathway. Your head should follow the movement of your shoulders. If this makes you dizzy, you may want to focus your eyes on a point in front of you.

If you are advanced, you can increase the effects of the exercise by standing on two Franklin Balls and imagining the kidneys and colon rotating with the lungs.

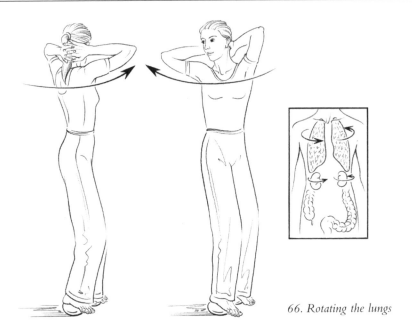

66. Rotating the lungs

The Kidneys

The kidneys are among the most important purification organs in the body. They fulfill their duties best when well supplied with blood. Fitness for the kidneys means sufficient fluid, above all drinking lots of (purified) water. Kidneys love warmth and should be protected on cold winter days and during sleep. Incidentally, the same warmth and fluid intake for the kidneys creates a vital and glowing appearance in the skin.

The kidney is an organ of regulation. It balances the components of the blood, regulates blood pressure, and maintains the correct acid-base balance.

Our two kidneys lie close to and on either side of the spine, at about the level of the upper lumbar vertebrae. The right kidney, because of the relative bulk of the liver above it, lies slightly lower than the left. The left ureter (the tube leading from the kidney to the urinary bladder) is thus a little longer than the right. A kidney weighs between 4.93 and 5.14 ounces (140 and 160 grams), is pearl colored and is surrounded by a connective tissue sac. This sac is attached to the diaphragm and the kidneys resemble ripe fruits hanging from it.

Because important nerves leading to the hip joints lie behind the kidneys, renal (kidney) problems may be a factor in hip pain. Tension and poor blood supply to the kidneys can also be a source of back pain.

The kidneys have an outer layer, the *renal cortex* and an inner core, the *renal medulla*. A number of three-sided, pyramid-shaped structures lead to the renal pelvis, where urine collects. From here urine flows downward through the ureters to the bladder. The bladder is a collecting tank for urine. It can hold between 1.5 and 2 quarts and is shaped like an inverted pyramid with an even-sided triangle as its roof.

The functional unit of the kidney is the *nephron*. The nephron includes long convoluted tubes and a structure called the *renal corpuscle* or *glomerulus*. The renal corpuscle is a filter; within it blood is channeled through winding capillaries supplied with filtering membranes. The capillaries are the initial filtering stations. Their inner walls have windows through which only certain materials can pass. These materials then arrive at the capillary's filtering membrane. This filter is composed of different layers and, like the inner capillary wall, allows certain materials to pass through while preventing others.

On the outside, and surrounding the capillary's filter membranes, are specialized cells called *podocytes*. Podocytes have extensions rather like an octopus (called *pedecils*, 'small feet') that wrap around, or embrace the capillary. The now-filtered blood is channeled between the arms of the podocytes.

The primary urine now moves through long thin tubes called *renal tubules*, where it is once again modified. The end product, actual urine, collects in the renal pelvis.

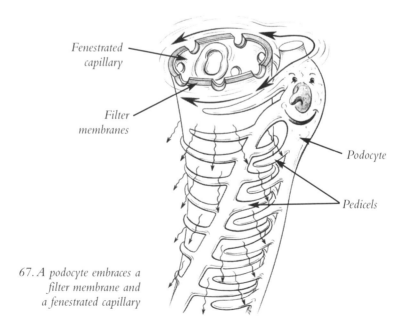

Fenestrated capillary

Filter membranes

Podocyte

Pedicels

67. A podocyte embraces a filter membrane and a fenestrated capillary

Making contact with the kidneys

Place your hands over the kidneys at the lower end of your ribs on your back. To reach them mentally, travel with your inner eye through the front of body and soft tissue for 4–5 inches, or from the back of the body for 3–4 inches.

Begin by following the movements of your breathing. To get a sense of the volume of the kidneys, visualize the space that they occupy. You can also let your imagination drift through and around this organ. Where do you experience clear contours and forms; where not? Where does the organ feel solid; where does it seem lax?

If inwardly you feel or see very little, it is important to have faith that images will come and to trust them when they do. With sufficient concentration, contact will be most certainly established. This contact generates an excellent foundation for kidney health.

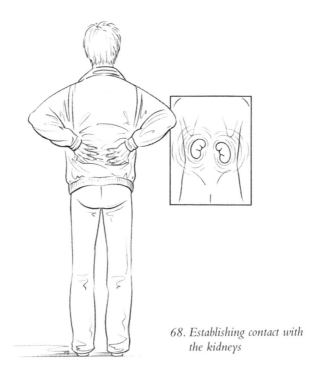

68. Establishing contact with the kidneys

The golden filter

Visualize the filter membrane of the kidney, embedded between capillary and podocyte. Think of the filters, the podocytes and the mesangial cells as beings that are alert and intelligent. Imagine that your perception influences the action of the filter. Your thoughts ensure that it functions at its best, and that the blood will be optimally purified. Imagine this purification not only as a mechanical event, but also as a mental process. Fluids collect information, then transport and deliver it. Picture the filter as it absorbs and sifts from the blood all unnecessary information, energy, and material.

While doing this, imagine that the blood has a golden light (or any color you wish). The light-invested blood facilitates all processes for every cell of every tissue. Imagine the filter glowing brightly, permeated and encased in glimmers of gold.

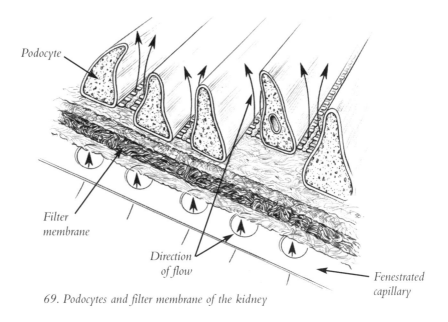

69. Podocytes and filter membrane of the kidney

A comprehensive perception of the kidneys influences our body´s flexibility. This will become more convincing when we perceive it in our own bodies.

Comparing a wooden and an elastic kidney

Slowly lift and lower your arms. How easily can this movement be performed? Lift your left and then the right knee, observing the ease of these movements.

Imagine that the kidneys are made of hardwood. Lift your arms and then the legs again. How do your limbs feel?

Now imagine blood flowing through the kidneys: the filters and all the kidney cells are working flexibly to purify the blood.

Lift your arms and legs once more. Do your limbs feel lighter?

The Liver

What the liver, lungs, and broccoli have in common

What could a head of broccoli and the liver possibly have in common? Both are *fractal forms*. Fractals arise through repeated multiplication, through the splitting of an existing form into smaller versions of the same form. An example is when a length is divided into three parts and each part in turn divided into three, and so on.

Trees, bushes and streams—there are countless fractal structures in nature. A tree fills to its best advantage the space available to it. Leaves are not crowded together, but seem by chance to find an ideal position from which to receive the most sunlight possible. When I look at a tree, I see no more than a green structure. But the tree's crown is made of individual leaves with space around each leaf. The tree's structure is created through an ever-finer and smaller repetition of the same dividing pattern. The entire assembly is a copy of single parts, and in the single part is revealed its overall form. As a result, there is optimal aeration and ample sunlight for all the leaves, and all available space is fully utilized. So the similarity between a tree and the lungs is perhaps more understandable. Through the fractal principle, we can see that the lungs create a large surface with which to make contact with air—about forty-three square feet per lung—in a very small space.

70. A natural fractal structure

How do fractals work? Let us consider the following problem. If the cell of a mouse were to generate exactly the same warmth as the cell of an elephant, and an elephant were to have many more cells and volume, but not much more surface space relative to the increase in cells that it possesses (100 times greater the surface and 10,000 times more cells than the mouse), then the elephant would die of heat stroke, and the mouse would freeze.

The mouse, because of its small volume, would have a complete blend of nutrients instantly available, while an elephant in the same situation would need a digestive eternity to receive the same kind of benefit from the food it ate. We know, though, that this is not actually the case. These two problems can be solved through fractals. Thus, an optimal mix of temperature and nutrition in a minimal body surface is achieved, and so too is optimal cooling with a maximum body surface. With the help of fractals, it is possible, without having endlessly long conduits, to reach every area of a structure.

Fractals offer a large advantage in temperature and fluid regulation within the body. The answer to the question of how blood reaches every cell without endlessly long vessels is because the vessels follow a set plan of becoming smaller and smaller. Thus, every place in the body is reached, without the blood having to travel great long distances back to the heart. An optimally functioning organ is uniformly fractal.

The largest gland in the body

The liver is the largest gland in the body. Every minute, 1.5 liters of blood flow through the liver. We have a total of 300 billion liver cells. In short, the liver analyses everything we have absorbed in the digestive tract. This is the final chance for detoxification before our blood enters regular circulation. The liver is therefore a buffer between our circulation, the entire inner environment of the body, and the outside world. If a poisonous substance succeeds in passing through the intestinal wall, the liver will catch it.

Alcohol travels directly to the liver and is toxic to cells because neither the intestines nor the liver can halt it completely. Alcohol also travels through the protective barrier to the brain (called the blood-brain barrier) because it resembles other substances found there. As a result, excessive alcohol is an anti-rejuvenation substance. The liver is also a reservoir for sugar, which is stored until it is needed in a form called *glycogen*.

You might want to visualize at least once the exact placement of the upper organs. Lie down and imagine the placement and form of the stomach and liver. Above the liver are the ribs and diaphragm. Behind the left section of the liver are the stomach and a part of the esophagus. To the right you will come to the gall bladder. Still further right is the large intestine, with the kidneys and adrenals above it. To the left and behind the liver is the stomach, and to the right the kidney.

The stomach, liver, and movements in breathing

With each breath, the diaphragm moves the stomach and the liver. On inhalation, the diaphragm moves downward. The stomach and liver are not able to get out of the way by moving to the back, so they move downward and are also stretched sideways. Relaxed and deep breathing is healthy for the organs because it stimulates their metabolism and circulation.

The cells of the liver (*hepatocytes*) have functions that are probably the most diverse in existence. They are polygon in form and are comparable to a *mandala*, (Sanskrit for 'circle') a symbol for unbroken unity that exists in many religions. The human liver is, in a definite sense, the plurality of a mandala.

Along with functions of detoxification, these cells also produce bile and plasma proteins. Plasma is blood without blood cells and is milky-white in color. Blood consists of plasma as well as white and red blood cells, and platelets. The white blood cells are immune cells, red blood cells transport oxygen, and platelets (*thrombocytes*) are responsible for preventing blood loss. Like the spleen, the liver recycles worn-out blood cells. It stores nutrients and also toxins (which can be a considerable problem). Toxins that cannot be immediately disposed of remain trapped in the liver. If the liver is not moving properly, its chemical functions suffer, which puts strain on the heart.

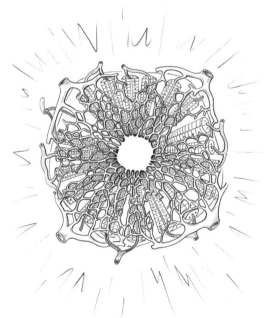

71. *Lobes of the liver*
as a mandala

The size and weight of the liver (about three pounds) can create serious difficulties. Because of its large mass, a small change in the liver's position can be the cause of massive changes in the overall equilibrium of the organ, and the infrastructure of connective tissue that separates and supports the abdominal organs. Problems associated with the liver include inflexibility in the thoracic vertebrae, imbalance in the neck and head, and problems with breathing when inflexibility forces the diaphragm to work harder.

An idealized image for the liver

Visualize a healthy liver: it is elastic, expandable, and well supplied with blood. It sits high up under the diaphragm, moves freely during respiration, and undertakes its metabolic duties with vigor.

Place your left hand at the front of your body at the level of your liver and your right hand on your back also at the level of your liver. Breathe into your liver and imagine the movement of this organ. Picture all the lobes operating flawlessly. Move the middle part of your back and imagine the liver being massaged by this movement. Now imagine it is the liver itself that is creating this movement.

The Digestive Tract

The digestive tract has several important functions. It is a highly effective defense organ: between fifty and sixty percent of lymphatic fluid originates in the digestive tract. Defense functions begin in the pharyngeal tonsils (adenoids) and the salivary glands, and extend as far as the small intestine, where an accumulation of white blood cells is found. Another function is the absorption of useable nutrients. Digestive mechanisms are controlled through the glandular functions of the intestine, and these are associated with the function of the 'abdominal brain' (see below.) Finally, the intestinal tract plays a role in relaxation, posture, flexibility, and coordination of movement.

A brain in the abdomen?

We are all familiar with butterflies in the stomach or 'gut instinct.' Although we might try very hard to make rationally-based decisions, it is often our gut feeling that most influences our behavior. This is because there are more nerves in the digestive tract than in the spinal cord. These nerves lie between the muscular layers of the intestine; combined they are called the *enteric nervous system*. In early animals, the nervous system was oriented to the mouth and the digestive tract. In humans this early brain still exists, but with a new function: simply formulated it coordinates not only digestive activity but also the dialogue between 'brain thinking' and 'gut thinking.' The 'power cord' linking these activities is the *vagus nerve*. In the same context we should remember that many illnesses have a psychosomatic origin. Through relaxation of the abdominal organs, we can quiet our thoughts and clearly consider our own behavior and functioning. Relaxing the gut frees us from stress.

Within the intestine, there are many messenger substances called *neuropeptides*. Relaxation increases the release of these substances. Feelings of well-being after eating arise from the presence of endorphins, which are neuropeptides. Eating under stress suppresses the production of these messenger materials.

To achieve relaxation in the intestines, imagine the double-layered wall of intestinal muscle. It is elastic and free. Imagine the intestine, lying calmly within the pelvis; sense its weight. This image can also be used while moving. Illustration 72 shows an elevated left leg and the pelvic basin, with a section of intestine called the *sigmoid colon* reposing comfortably within.

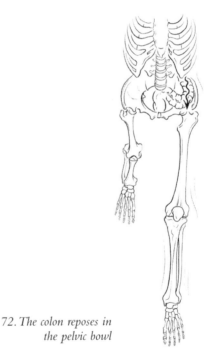

72. The colon reposes in the pelvic bowl

Digestion

Digestion begins with the eyes and nose. We think a great deal before we eat something. How will it taste? Motivation and appetite are crucial. The mouth has a lot to do with yearning and falling in love, hence the popularity of kissing. In fact, kissing for rejuvenation is highly recommended!

Food is broken into small pieces in the mouth and mixed with saliva. If we do this carefully, we make a further contribution to the health of the digestive system.

The salivary glands are *exocrine glands*, meaning they are glands which release substances into ducts, in this case the digestive tract. *Endocrine glands* release substances into the blood. (The pancreas is the exception, being both an endocrine and an exocrine organ.) Visualizing food before we eat facilitates the flow of saliva, which in turn makes digestion possible. Thus 'eating' food mentally (in advance) aids digestion and limits intake since mentally one has already ingested. Dieting begins with the power of suggestion, for example, when you can accurately envision your ideal weight. If you can see yourself on the scales at your ideal weight, and imagine others noticing your slimmer figure, then you will be well on the way to reaching this goal. Many people who are unsuccessful invest more mental energy in what they wish to *avoid* than in the goal of slenderness.

The esophagus

The trachea, or windpipe, is an open structure like a tube, while the esophagus is more like a hose. Awareness of the windpipe and the esophagus can help relieve neck tension. In your imagination travel down the esophagus, which is normally closed.

A narrow space allows the esophagus to pass through the diaphragm. Muscles contract to actively narrow sections of the digestive tract—they are called sphincters. The mouth, the stomach outlet, the entrance to the large intestine, and the anus are examples of sphincter muscles. The sphincters are controls in the hose-like structure of the digestive system.

The stomach

The stomach is a test chamber for food. This is the final site where anything harmful can be ejected. Enzymatic breakdown of food also takes place in the stomach. The entrance to the stomach is a little to the left of the body's midline.

The stomach has three layers of muscle; the innermost is arranged in multiple folds and is lined with a thick layer of mucous. Stress can damage this layer, allowing toxic material to enter the body through the stomach and intestinal walls—a further argument for the use of relaxation and imagination.

The small intestine

The stomach releases food bit by bit into the intestine, but only as much as can be digested. This is controlled by a gateway at the stomach's lower portion called the *pyloric sphincter*. Food is moved into the duodenum (the name means 'twelve' as the duodenum in length is the approximate width of twelve fingers), where food particles are further subdivided into nutritional building blocks that can be absorbed. After passing through the duodenum, food enters the small intestine, a structure about twenty feet long, where ninety percent of it will be absorbed.

The small intestine contains structures called *villi*, which look rather like small fingers. The villi enlarge the absorbent surface of the intestine so greatly that an area of just under 1,100 square feet, about the size of a tennis court, is achieved. The villi have a thin membrane that is regularly renewed, about nine ounces daily. When new cells appear at the base of the villi, they migrate quickly and the cells they replace are shed from the tip.

In the small intestine, these cells trap amino acids and digest them. The small intestine is where nutrition takes place, unless the intestine is obstructed, in which case intestinal cleansing is helpful. Not only chemical compounds are absorbed, but also water and minerals. Between the villi, cells called *enteroendocrine cells* are embedded, which produce hormones and mucous.

The large intestine (cecum, colon, rectum, anus)

Food ultimately enters the large intestine via the *ileocecal valve*. It is important that these connections function well. When we are stressed, all the sphincters tighten up.

The *cecum* is at the beginning of the large intestine and is basically a big pouch about 2.5 inches long that receives waste material from the small intestine. Within it, bacteria break down cellulose and other material difficult to process. The cecum is a kind of blind alley, or cul de sac, which functions as our own internal compost box. The *vermiform* (worm) *appendix* (appendage), a lymphatic organ, hangs from it.

We have an ascending, a transverse, and a descending colon. The descending colon extends downward into the pelvic basin, where it becomes the sigmoid (S-shaped) portion. The *sigmoid colon* extends backward to the tailbone and becomes the rectum, the final portion of which is the anus. Here there is an inner involuntary sphincter, as well as an outer voluntary sphincter that we can control. A baby does not have control yet over the outer sphincter and thus empties the intestine freely.

Intestinal motion

Imagine the longitudinal and circular muscles of the intestine, and how they move. The movement of digestion is called *peristalsis* and is somewhat like squeezing the last bit of toothpaste through the tube.

Intestinal tissue also has its own motion, like seaweed waving to and fro. The intestine as a whole moves with the rhythm of breathing and its motion is connected to the movement of our entire body. The villi stretch out into the intestinal space to absorb nutrients—collectively a true symphony of movement that we are usually never aware of.

Tapping over the intestines

One of the simplest yet most effective exercises is to gently tap over the digestive organs. Tap on the entire stomach/intestinal area in the direction of digestive movement. Begin over the cecum, at the front right side of the pelvis. From there, move up to the ribs, then to the left across the transverse colon to the stomach and down along the descending colon. Tap once more and imagine the release of the intestinal muscles; the villi will be shaken gently as they receive new blood and produce messengers of well-being.

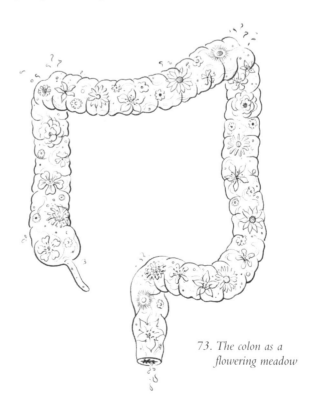

73. *The colon as a flowering meadow*

To conclude, continue to tap over the area of the small intestine and around the navel. Say inwardly, "My intestine is relaxed, strong, and healthy. Every nutrient will be optimally absorbed. My intestine renews itself daily."

Afterward, stroke over the ascending and descending colon, continuing downward to your legs, in order to perceive the connection between the colon and the legs. Hold a large sponge over the ascending colon to convey a sense of the organs. Bend forward to feel how the sponge folds. It is an external aid with which to better sense your internal environment. Notice the expanding elasticity of the sponge as you roll upright. Imagine the intestine compressing and expanding like a sponge.

Complete your picture with the image of a colon that feels healthy, flexible, and as fresh as a colorful spring meadow.

Chapter 7: The Glands

Glands are classified as organs, but for purposes of clarity they will have their own chapter.

Hormones regulate metabolic processes in the body. The glandular activity producing these hormones is therefore closely associated with the aging process. Time and again over the past centuries, herbal aids or animal extracts have been sought for hormone production, above all to replace or stimulate production of estrogen and androgen (the female and male sex hormones). Such substances often came from disagreeable sources and were administered in disagreeable ways, an example being the injection of extracts from animal testicles. To this day, all over the world, sexually stimulating substances are sought. But the cheapest, safest and most effective stimulant of all resides in the power of the imagination.

The Thyroid and Human Growth Hormone

If you can find the top of the larynx (the voicebox, at the bottom of the neck) and gently press the soft tissue below it, you will find the thyroid.

Thyroxine is produced in the thyroid and regulates cellular metabolic activity, a growth hormone *par excellence*. A decrease in this hormone lowers the metabolism; you feel limp and without vitality. Metabolism includes the cellular chemical processes within the body that are responsible for tissue growth and regeneration, and for converting energy into processes needed to sustain life. Studies have determined that the production of thyroxine in the thyroid of older adults does not normally decrease. The same research has shown that cells cannot always recognize this hormone even when it is present in normal amounts. Whether thyroxine (because it stimulates energy, regeneration, and growth) is a 'wonder drug' for rejuvenation is a hot topic.

The best solution is still to create the hormone naturally in everyday behavior, so that it will be naturally distributed. Imagination, movement, and healthy nutrition all help. Growth hormone, for example, is circulated in the blood in response to strength training.

Expression and the thyroid

Because the thyroid gland rests on the windpipe (trachea), it is massaged when we speak. In the same way that there are very pleasant and conversely much less pleasant massages, so too with speech and the thyroid. The thyroid likes the vibrations of congenial words. It also likes the kind of firm massage that results when we express ourselves clearly and are steady, with both feet on the floor. Notice your thyroid the next time you speak. You will perceive that your speech alters and that you are conscious of maintaining clarity. Imagining the cooling, soothing color blue is helpful for the thyroid; an image of a fluttering (blue) butterfly is also helpful. This is because the thyroid should not stick to the windpipe but lie loosely like a silk shawl.

A bright "aaa…" (the long vowel sound as in the word *made*) sets the thyroid vibrating and activates it. An overactive thyroid can be calmed with gentle images. Mental dialogue with the thyroid is very beneficial.

The Adrenals and Adrenalin

The adrenals are glands that are also important for feelings of vitality. The right adrenal is pyramid-shaped and touches the liver. The left is more rounded. The adrenals are two to three inches long, half an inch to an inch wide and about two inches thick. They consist of an outer layer (*cortex*) and an inner core (*medulla*). The adrenals sit like little caps on the kidneys, but have nothing to do with them directly.

Hormones produced in the adrenals modify our response to stress, which is an important factor in aging. People who have reached a very advanced age claim ability to weather adverse circumstances with composure. It is also a fact that the ability to produce adrenal hormones does not diminish with age. I mention these examples of long-term and well-functioning organs in order to challenge the pervasive belief that age and decay must somehow be partners. For many areas of the body, there is simply no proof for this. However, life-long negative behavior shows up in aging of, for instance, the bones, joints, and locomotor system overall. One of the most important and easily learned techniques for rejuvenation is the aforementioned postural training. (You will find those exercises in Chapter 4 on bones and Chapter 5 on joints.) Posture is also related to the glands. If these are full of vitality, they keep our posture upright. Studies have even shown that symmetry in posture is one of the most attractive features for the opposite sex.

Relaxing the adrenals

Visualize one of your adrenals sitting like a small cap on the kidney. Imagine it relaxing as if it were a small hot water bottle covered in fleece. The warmth is felt by the kidneys, delighted to have such comforting neighbors above. Say to the adrenals, "Please produce the exact amount of hormones my body requires: not too few and not too many. And please stay relaxed at all times."

The Pituitary—the Master Gland

Situated just below the brain, the pituitary gland is often called the master gland. It produces hormones that control other glands, among which are the thyroid, adrenals, ovaries, and testes. At this time there are no reliable studies demonstrating that pituitary function lessens with age. The pituitary hangs like a small berry on a stem from the *hypothalamus*, from which it in turn receives signals regarding which hormones to release.

The hormonal dance

Touch the place between your eyebrows and travel in your thoughts behind this point, which is also called the 'third eye.' Visualize the pituitary, like a drop of dew on a leaf. Visualize the pituitary scattering its hormones so that all the glands under

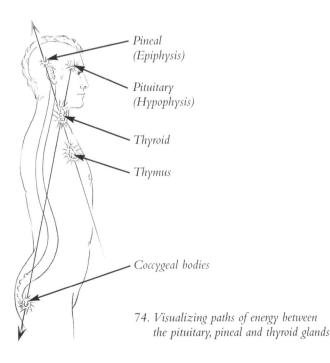

Pineal
(Epiphysis)

Pituitary
(Hypophysis)

Thyroid

Thymus

Coccygeal bodies

74. *Visualizing paths of energy between the pituitary, pineal and thyroid glands*

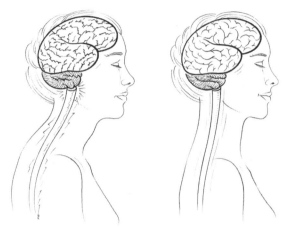

75. *A heavy brain compresses the spinal cord; a light brain straightens it*

its control are harmonized. This is like a courtly dance between the pituitary, thyroid, adrenals, and ovaries or testes.

The hormonal interactions between glands might be visualized as directed arrows or pathways. Visualize these inter-glandular connections as highways along which communication between glands takes place.

Thanks to its placement behind the forehead, the pituitary is the gland of body verticality and alignment, and is related to carriage of the spine and the head. If you have never thought about aligning your brain, the time has now come. This is helpful because a heavy brain makes life difficult and compresses the spinal cord (the thought alone is perceptively negative).

Children are often picture-perfect examples of a floating pituitary and a 'lifted brain.'

76. *The lifted, yet supple carriage of a child's head*

Floating and upright

Imagine the pituitary as a tiny balloon, lifting the head and brain. It imparts the feeling of a string attached to the head drawing us upward, which can also be practiced in challenging exercises for balance.

The Pancreas and Insulin

The pancreas lies below the stomach and above the duodenum (the first section of the small intestine). It is about six inches long and consists of a tail and a head. It lies diagonally in the upper abdomen: from behind, left, and above; to the front, middle, and below. At the end of its tail on the upper left is the spleen. At its other end on the lower right the head lies in the curling loop of the duodenum, as if it were a pillow.

The part of the pancreas with endocrine function is made up of a million cell clusters called the *islets of Langerhans*. These secrete insulin into the blood. Insulin regulates sugar metabolism. Also produced in the pancreas are about one and a half quarts of digestive juices. When we are tense, nervous, and stressed, we secrete very little digestive juice. The intestinal tract dries up and digestion is difficult.

Factors that influence the pancreas

Whether the reduction of insulin production in increasing age is a foreshadowing of diabetes or is truly a part of aging, is unclear. On the other hand, the pancreas is influenced by three factors already known to us: imagery, movement, and nutrition. The causes of diabetes in the Western world are lack of physical activity and being overweight, first and foremost. A great deal of mental discipline is needed to change eating habits, to haul oneself off the sofa, turn off the television, and begin to practice rejuvenating exercises.

For weight loss, I recommend applying crystal-clear goal setting, using motivational images and self-conversation. The belief and trust that everything is possible works wonders. You might reflect on what life would be like if you knew you could reach every goal you set. Your conversation with yourself can be: "I can achieve my goals. I can picture myself at an ideal weight. I sense myself fit, as if I were in shape. I can experience the response of those around me, as if I had already reached my objective."

Posture and the pancreas

It is astonishing that with help from the pancreas, you can coordinate movement interactions between the arms, legs, head, and torso. A geometric relationship can be visualized between the pancreas and the body's extremities.

Stand up and stroke with your right hand over the pancreas, from under the sternum downward to your left leg. Picture a fluid connection made by doing this.

Now stroke with your right hand from the pancreas along your left arm to your left hand. Repeat these two sequences several times—from the pancreas to your left leg and then from the pancreas to your left hand.

Next, stand on your left leg with your left arm stretched upward. Pulse a little on your supporting knee, sensing your back release as you balance. To compare, now stand on your right leg—you will feel less stable. Your back will be less released and your balance not as good as on the left.

Repeat the stroking sequences on the right side. Stroke with your left hand down your right leg to your foot, then along your right arm to the right hand. Repeat this several times. You will feel better balanced, your posture easy and upright. Sense the pancreas as your postural center.

The Thymus

The thymus lies right behind the sternum, just above and counterbalancing the heart. In infancy and childhood the thymus is larger than the heart itself. Later on, the thymus shrinks, although it remains an exceedingly important organ for the immune system. The heart, incidentally, also practices endocrine functions. The thymus is the training and education center for *T cells* (lymphocytes). Along with the spleen, lymph nodes, and digestive tract, the thymus is one of the most important organs in the immune system. A small child's thymus is larger than an adult's because childhood is when training for the immune system is needed. As adults, we often neglect the thymus by slumping our upper body, so that the sternum presses onto this delicate organ. The cellular construction of the thymus is fascinating. It is here we find 'nurse cells,' cells surrounding an entire group of lymphocytes (immune cells), thus displaying a cellular example of affectionate embrace.

An "Aaah" for the amazing thymus

When we vocalize a clear "Aaah…", and certainly when we sing, we cause the thymus to vibrate—which also encourages blood circulation and other positive activity. Place a hand on the upper part of the sternum, where you can feel vibration of the voice. With a clear "Aaah…" to activate the heart and thymus, stroke from their upper region outward along your arm. The vocalization opens and expands the sternum, which improves shoulder alignment and relaxes the muscles in the shoulder and neck.

The above experience shows that mindful vocalizing and imagery for the thymus helps us to relax, to bring pleasure and ease. This is also true for the hands and finger joints when typing on a computer.

The Pineal and Reproductive Glands

The pineal gland (*epiphysis cerebri*) controls the body's day/night rhythms through secretion and distribution of the hormone melatonin. Light falling on the eyes during the day prevents the hormone from entering the blood. At night, the absence of light causes melatonin to be distributed and promotes sleep. Melatonin is also thought to be a 'rejuvenation pill' because it improves sleep rhythms, strengthens the immune system, and arms the body against stress.

Activating melatonin

The pineal is the uppermost and most posteriorly positioned gland. It lies deep in the brain between the two halves of the thalamus. To locate it, touch the back of your head and visualize diagonally forward and down, into the deepest part of the brain.

For a deep regenerative sleep, imagine that the pineal delivers melatonin at your mental bidding. (But please, only after you have set this book aside!)

The Sex Hormones

The production of sex hormones diminishes with age, according to scientific studies. Even so, our attitude and behavior can have a decisive influence on this process. For example, sexual activity for men can decrease from four times a week at age twenty to once a week after age sixty. A good way to boost the sex hormones is to practice the former amount of activity at the latter age. According to a book by the German author Manfred Twrznik, sexual interest for women increases with age while it decreases for men. From this point of view, the key to increased production of sex hormones for both men and women is obvious, namely by acceding to the desires of women (including foreplay which stimulates the hormones).

Chapter 8: The Brain and Nervous System

The brain is the approximate size of a grapefruit, looks something like a cauliflower, and weighs about as much. The brain consists of approximately a 100,000,000 neurons, or nerve cells, and the number of connections possible between them is greater than the atoms in the entire universe.

Changes in the brain with advancing years are not remarkable. Certainly some cells are lost, but the number of brain cells is so enormous that the loss scarcely affects brain function. Because a precise explanation is not yet available of the processes in the brain responsible for memory, a few cells that go missing can scarcely be held to account for memory deterioration. A further study showed the brain at age 64 to have become somewhat smaller, but that memory and attention were not affected. It has also been shown that our brain can produce new cells throughout our entire life. This has been shown to take place in the *hippocampus*, an area of the brain that is responsible for turning short term into long-term memories, but there also seem to be stem cells capable of reproduction in other areas of the brain (see Doidge, M., 2007, *The Brain that Changes Itself*, p. 251. New York: Penguin Books).

Neurons react with great sensitivity to reduced oxygen. The loss of neurons is not due to cell death but to disease processes in the vessels (*arteriosclerosis*), too little exercise, and smoking. The brain has an enormous reserve and thus it is that 100-year-old-people are often very clear thinkers, especially if the body and the brain are exercised regularly.

Imagery as Brain Training

Activity practiced daily rejuvenates the brain, just as it rejuvenates the muscles. This does not necessarily mean that we have to solve math problems every day (although it is not a bad idea); it means that in general we should practice the special functions of the brain daily. Imagination is doubly suitable in this regard because imagery alone exercises the brain. At the same time, the contents of the image can have additional healthy effects.

Fat is healthy

This heading might seem surprising, but as far as neurons are concerned, fat is in fact very healthy stuff. We are not referring to fat under the skin but to a protective sheath consisting mostly of fat (lipid) that surrounds most *axons*. (Axons are the long part of the nerve along which a nerve impulse travels.) In the central nervous system (the brain and spinal cord) and in the peripheral nervous system (cranial and spinal nerves) are cells whose job it is to wind themselves around the nerves in order to protect, nourish, and enhance their conductivity. These cells are called *neuroglia* (literally, 'nerve glue'). Two examples of these are *oligodentrocytes* and *astrocytes*, neuroglia of the brain and spinal cord. Neuroglia elsewhere in the body are called *Schwann cells*.

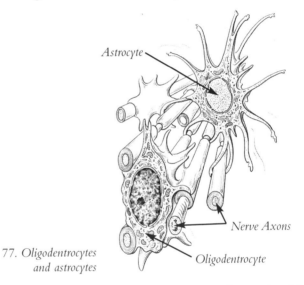

Astrocyte

Nerve Axons

77. *Oligodentrocytes and astrocytes*

Oligodentrocyte

When neuroglia are healthy, the nerves function well. But should the neuroglia break down or vanish, a number of diseases can arise, the most familiar being multiple sclerosis. The protective sheath with which the neuroglia surrounds the nerve consists of a type of fat called *myelin*.

Protection for the nerve axons

Visualize the myelin and the nerve axon. This protective sheath can be plump and full. Imagine this protective carrier as a pillow for the neuron. Picture how this covering insulates, protects, and nourishes. Thanks to neuroglia, the conduction and function of the brain and of the entire nervous system become sharper, stronger, and better. Inwardly say, "My nerves are ably protected and are well supplied with nutrient-rich blood. With every breath I sustain my nerves with oxygen; they become ever more resilient and durable."

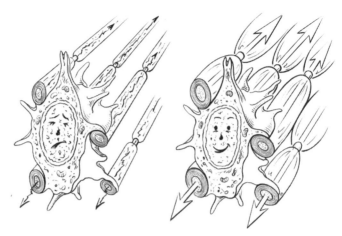

78. Scant myelin encases the axon on the left; plentiful myelin on the right

Nerves should be protected, suspended within their sheaths, and well supplied with nutrients. They must also be able to function unhindered by foreign material or residue. Diseases such as Alzheimer's show up in patches called plaques or in other deposits and appear to accompany an impairment of brain function.

A clear view for the nervous system

Imagine these plaques being scrubbed away by a devoted brigade of cleaning personnel. Imagine the nerve axons freed of any plaque and disabling material. Picture

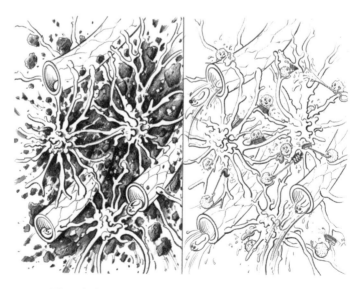

79. Left: deposits in the brain. Right: cleaning the brain

mini-vacuum cleaners removing everything undesirable. The nerve cells have a clear view of one another and open communication. Visualize a brain and nervous system that are clean, clear and able to communicate.

Schwann cells, collagen, and connective tissue sheaths

As we know, relaxation heals and regenerates. And the nerve cells with their axon extensions need as much stimulation to relax as the muscles and organs. It is also true that nerves do not usually exist as naked forms, but have support structures of various kinds surrounding them. There are nerves with only a small protective layer and slower conductivity. A typical 'fast' nerve is accompanied by collagen fibers in a connective tissue covering, protecting it against compression and over-stretching, as well as the already familiar myelin sheath that boosts conductivity and also has nutritive and regenerative functions. If a nerve is injured, it is the myelin that regenerates first, laying down a tube for the regenerating nerve to grow into. Once again we see an example of teamwork, without which the body could not function.

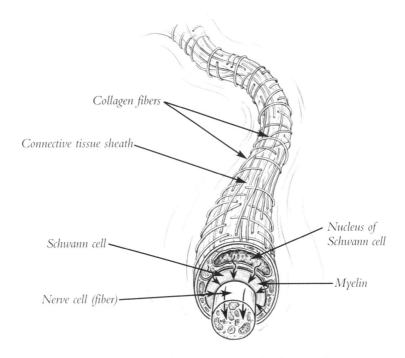

Collagen fibers

Connective tissue sheath

Schwann cell

Nerve cell (fiber)

Nucleus of
Schwann cell

Myelin

*80. Neuronal process (axon) with Schwann cell,
connective tissue, and collagen casing*

Relaxation for the nerves

Imagine that, within their protective sheaths, the nerve axons relax in a bed of down. Everyone knows what it feels like to recline on a soft bed. Transfer this image to your nerves. They lie as calm and relaxed as babies within their protective sheaths. Sense all the nerve axons in the body lying comfortably, sighing as they enjoy such grand relaxation.

81. A nerve relaxing in its sheath

Nerves sway in the wind

Stand upright and sense the nerves extending from the brainstem and spinal cord to the entire body. Lengthening like a host of delicate branches, they are able to reach the most distant corners of the body. Slowly drop forward by bending your back one vertebra at a time until you reach the floor. Bend the legs slightly and allow the head and arms to hang.

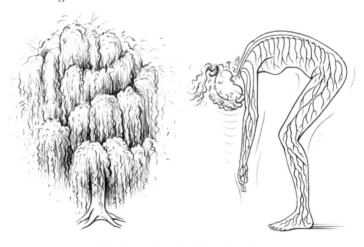

82. Nerves hanging like willow boughs

Imagine all your nerves loose and relaxed within their tissue sheaths, completely released like the boughs of a willow. Let the boughs and the leaves sway gently to and fro. Then slowly straighten the spine, nerve-by-nerve, until you are upright. Sense the nerves embedded softly in supportive tissue.

Individual neurons communicate with help from contact points called *synapses*. At the synapses, information is conveyed along chemical paths from one neuron to the next. Substances that bridge the space between one neuron and the next are called *neurotransmitters*. The amount and quality of neurotransmitters have a large effect on the functioning of the brain. Imagine that the best quality neurotransmitters and motivational messages will be passed from one synapse to another. Synapses can end at other synapses, at a nerve axon, or at a nerve body. Imagine that these connections are supported and improved by your ability to visualize. Set a goal to uphold and improve these connections in the brain through mental ability and learning.

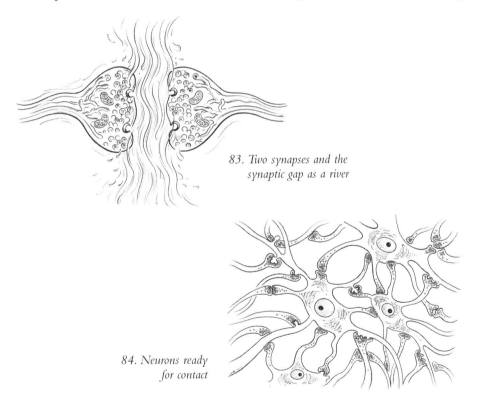

83. Two synapses and the synaptic gap as a river

84. Neurons ready for contact

One of the most important neurotransmitters in the brain is *acetylcholine*. A decrease can bring about diverse illnesses. Imagine that your brain faithfully produces and keeps in circulation plenty of acetylcholine. Say inwardly, "My brain makes all the necessary neurotransmitters available in the correct amounts."

Dynamic brain

Thanks to clear goals and training in the use of imagery, we can be assured that our brain is able, not only to maintain its resilience, but even to develop it over the years. The brain is active and dynamic, adaptable and creative; it is untiring in its constant striving to progress and grow.

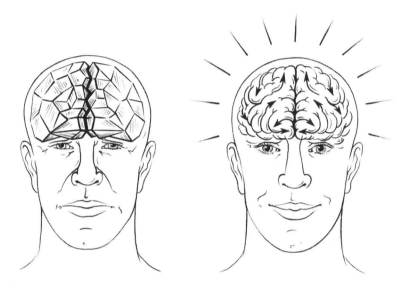

85. From the (left) blocked to the (right) dynamic brain

The 10-Day Beauty Program

This program is unusual, *because the emphasis is on your mental attitude and imagination, closely tied with physical action, as the foundation for beauty, youthfulness, and health.* You can use these exercises in your daily life, anywhere you are. You can practice marvelously, even on a bus or airplane. Show your body that you mean it—and you will find that you will stick with it! The short-term goals are to improve general well-being, appearance, flexibility, and an optimistic outlook over a period of ten days.

Track your progress on the chart at the end.

First Day

1

A dialogue with the face

1. Place your hands on your face and say inwardly,

"My face radiates beauty and ease, my lips radiate beauty and ease, my eyes radiate beauty and ease…"

A dialogue with the body

2. Sit or lie comfortably and say to yourself,

"My joints inhale the sense of relaxed well-being. My bones are flexible and strong, my muscles are powerful and supple, my organs are healthy and well-supplied with blood, my skin is pliant and beautiful, my nerves are calm and relaxed, my entire body radiates beauty and ease."

Posture

3. Stand on a rolled towel or Franklin Balls (see Appendix for information) without shoes. Balance on the towel so that your toes can move. Initially hold on to something stable. As you get more practiced, you can stand without holding on and stretch your arms overhead.

Imagine that your head floats upward like a helium-filled balloon.

Whoever works in an office...

...should practice standing up and sitting down 10 times, several times a day with a "long feeling" in the back and good use of the hip joint. (See the illustration.) Begin slowly and then speed up. This is an excellent leg, abdomen, and back exercise. You will sit taller afterward!

Abdomen and back

4. Wrap an elastic band (or Thera-Band®; see Appendix for more information) behind your back and hold it firmly in your hands. Pushing against the band, move your back flexibly to the back, then to the left, and to the right. Breathe!

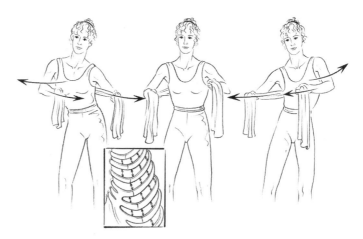

Fasten the elastic band to a stable place behind you. Sit on a stool, feet on the floor, and hold the ends of the band. Rotate the torso to the right and to the left, extending alternate arms to the front. Breathe deeply.

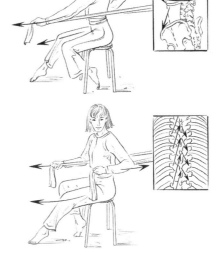

Shoulder and neck release

At the first sign of tension in the neck and shoulders, perform the **shoulder-as-sponge** exercise.

5. Place your right hand on the left shoulder (arm in front), near your neck where the muscles are more thickly layered. Make small

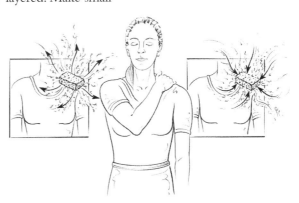

circles with the left shoulder. Because the shoulder is 70% water, and water is, of course, fluid, make the circles as if watching water ebb and flow in response to the movement. Now circle the shoulder in the other direction, noticing that your breathing is becoming more peaceful. With the right hand in the same place on the relaxed shoulder, gently squeeze the muscles with the fingers as if squeezing a sponge. Imagine all tension in the shoulder being squeezed out through this 'sponge'. Now release the fingers and then the entire hand. Slowly let go of the sponge, and imagine water flowing back as it is reabsorbed while the muscle sponge fills out and spreads and widens.

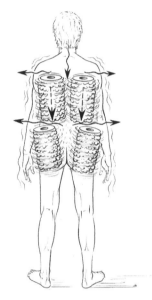

Do this imagery exercise to loosen the back:

6. Imagine two spools of fluffy wrap-around wash mops, similar to those in an automated carwash but smaller. These spools release tension from the posterior side of your body. They spiral slowly down the back from the shoulder blades to the pelvis. The outward rolling of the mops expands the back further; the downward spiraling conveys a sense of increasing length. Feelings of spaciousness develop in your back aided by deep breathing, right into the cells.

Before going to sleep...

...allow all the good things that took place over the day to run through your head. Imagine that tomorrow will be pleasant and rewarding.

Second Day

2

Read through your goals and perhaps expand them.

1. Repeat the exercises from the first day with these modifications:

Stand and sit 11 times.

Using an elastic band sit and rotate the torso 11 times with alternate arms pushing to the front.

The focus for the day

On this day focus on **everything going smoothly**, both in your body and in your mind. Imagine your thoughts to be silky and smooth and your joints to be well lubricated and flexible. Whenever you perform a movement focus on how smoothly you are doing the action and embody the fact that your joints are benefiting from this movement. It can be the most simple thing, like reaching for the coffee pot or for a book.

Use this opportunity to make your joints feel flexible and healthy. This takes no time investment at all, since you are practicing flexibility during movements you will be doing anyhow. Think the following thought: "Today everything is going very smoothly, and, if ever I feel any tension, I will remind myself to revert to my smooth and flexible state."

Take care of your joints

To take care of your joints, it is helpful to visualize how cartilage is constructed. (Cartilage is material at the ends of the bones, allowing the joint to resist pressure and provide optimal gliding. Its surface ensures the nearly frictionless movement of both ends of the bone.) Thin threads of collagen within the cartilage are arranged in an arch-like fashion, as the arch is a structure capable of supporting extremely heavy loads.

2. Do this exercise for the knee joint:

Standing up, imagine the myriad arches of cartilage supporting you. These arches are very elastic and smooth, and very strong. Perform small bouncing movements with your legs and imagine the living cartilage arches elastically bending and springing back.

Third Day

3

1. Repeat the exercises from the second day with the following modifications:

Stand and sit 12 times.

Using an elastic band, sit and rotate the torso 12 times with alternate arms pushing to the front.

2. Over the course of the day, place your hand over your heart and breathe into it. Allow the heart to float.

The focus for the day

Today you will focus on **muscle sliding**. Whenever you perform a movement think of the muscle filaments sliding smoothly past each other. Choose to focus on muscle sliding during very mundane movements—that is the key to moving your body rapidly to a more youthful state.

Do not postpone feeling good in your body just to get some work done faster. In fact, if you focus on muscle sliding you will get the work done faster and feel good as well. If you have a very tight spot simply place your hand on it and slowly squeeze the tension out of the area using the sponge image (see above, First Day). When you let go of your grip imagine water flowing into the muscle as sponge to cause a sense of spacious relaxation.

3. Lie on the ground, your fingers laced behind your head. This protects the neck from strain and keeps it as relaxed as possible. When lifting the head, shoulders and upper body, concentrate on the internal gliding-together of the rectus abdominus muscle. The top of the sternum reaches toward the pelvis as the alternating muscle filaments slide together. At all times, the neck harmonizes with the lengthening torso.

Slow down the movement as you lower your back to the ground. This will increase your strength gains.

Here is an exercise for the deltoid muscle using the muscle sliding image. (The deltoid is attached on the upper arm and the outside of the shoulder. It assists in lifting the arm).

4. Place the right hand lightly on the left deltoid muscle. Lift the left arm to the front and imagine the muscle filaments beneath the right hand sliding past each other. Repeat the movement seven times, with the same image. Now lift both arms together and compare the ease of the movement. Notice that the arm you moved previously feels lighter and more mobile. Repeat the exercise on the other side.

Fourth Day

4

1. Repeat all the exercises from the previous day with the following modifications:

Stand and sit 13 times with self-talk: "My muscles are supple, strong and beautiful; my joints are well lubricated."

Using an elastic band, rotate the torso 13 times with alternate arms pushing forward, while visualizing your ideal abdomen.

The focus for the day

Today will be your day for **strengthening the abdominal muscles**.

2. Lie on your back with your arms relaxed on the floor next to your torso, and lift your feet, one after the other, from the floor, so that your knee aims for the chest. The back remains on the floor. The knees do not straighten, but stay relaxed.

Visualize the transverse abdominal muscle and sense how it holds the lower back in its supportive grip. Repeat the movement 20 times, moving loosely and breathing rhythmically with the movement of your legs. Return your feet to the floor and note that your back will feel expansive and more relaxed.

You can increase your strength each week by doing 4 extra leg lifts, until several weeks later you have reached about 50 repeats.

Fifth Day

5

1. Repeat all the exercises from the previous day with these modifications:

Stand and sit 14 times with self-talk: "My muscles are supple and strong; my joints are well lubricated." To ensure that your shoulders are relaxed, place your hands in your armpits and imagine the armpits to be deep and soft.

Sitting down, using an elastic band rotate the torso 14 times with alternate arms pushing forward, while visualizing your ideal abdomen.

2. Three times over the course of the day, imagine how the glands distribute the correct amount of hormones needed for health and beauty. This exercise is for the adrenal glands, which are located near the liver and kidneys. Hormones produced in the adrenals are important for feelings of vitality and modify our response to stress. Production of these hormones does not diminish with age!

3. Visualize one of your adrenals sitting like a small cap on the kidney. Imagine it relaxing as if it were a small hot water bottle covered in fleece. The kidneys, delighted to have such comforting neighbors above, feel the warmth. Say to the adrenals, "Please produce the exact amount of hormones my body requires: not too few and not too many. And please stay relaxed at all times."

The focus for the day

Today you will focus on **organ health**.

4. Place your right hand on your left lung next to your breastbone (sternum) and your left hand on your left kidney (lower back). Keep your shoulders relaxed as you focus on your breathing. Imagine both your lungs and kidneys filling with fresh oxygen as you inhale. Feel both organs relax as you exhale. Repeat the image 7 times, then remove your hands.

Take a moment to notice the difference between the left and right side of your body. The left side will be more relaxed and your breathing will be deeper, too. Now repeat on the right side. Imagine both your lungs and kidneys filling with fresh oxygen as you inhale. Feel both organs relax as you exhale. Repeat the image seven times.

Sixth Day

1. Repeat all the exercises from the previous day with these modifications:

Stand and sit 15 times with self-talk: "My muscles are supple and strong, my joints are well lubricated."

With an elastic band, rotate the torso 15 times with alternate arms pushing forward, while visualizing your ideal abdomen.

The focus for the day

Today is your **heart day**.

2. Four times during the day, place a hand on your heart and breathe into the heart. Allow the heart to float.

3. Lie with your legs elevated. Contract your leg muscles to assist the veins with the helpful movement of the muscles. Imagine the venous valves becoming stronger and transporting blood to the heart with sufficient vigor. Relax your legs and shake them lose. Alternate contracting and relaxing the legs 5 times, then lower them and relax completely. The strength of the return flow relieves the heart and allows it to beat more softly.

4. Place the palm of your right hand on the area slightly to the left of your sternum at the bottom of the ribcage. Imagine your heart to be beating with joy and ease sending "happy blood" through your body. Think of your heart literally as a rejuvenation and motivational center for your blood. No matter how silly it may seem at first, imagine the blood emerging from your heart to be bright, smiling and vigorous. Think of your blood being eager to enter the heart. Imagine a happy and balanced relationship between your heart and your blood.

Seventh Day

7

1. Repeat all the exercises from the previous day with the following modifications:

Stand and sit 16 times with self-talk: "My muscles are supple and strong; my joints are well lubricated."

Using an elastic band, rotate the torso 16 times with alternate arms pushing forward, while visualizing your ideal flat stomach.

2. It is astonishing that with help from the pancreas, you can coordinate movement interactions between the arms, legs, head and torso. Do this interactive imagery exercise for posture, and practice it for 3 minutes:

(The pancreas lies below the stomach and above the duodenum, the first section of the small intestine. A part of it secretes insulin into the blood, which regulates sugar metabolism.)

Stand up and stroke with your right hand over the pancreas, from under the sternum downward to your left leg. Picture a fluid connection made by doing this.

Now stroke with your right hand from the pancreas along your left arm to your left hand. Repeat these two sequences several times—from the pancreas to your left leg and then from the pancreas to your left hand.

Next, stand on your left leg with your left arm stretched upward. Pulse a little on your supporting knee, sensing your back release as you balance. To compare, now stand on your right leg—you will feel less stable. Your back will be less released and your balance not as good as on the left.

Repeat the stroking sequences on the right side. Stroke with your left hand down your right leg to your foot, then along your right arm to the right hand. Repeat this several times. You will feel better balanced, your posture easy and upright. Sense the pancreas as your postural center.

The focus for the day

Today is your **motivational day**. Take a moment to imagine what you really like to do even if you cannot do it at the moment. Visualize your favorite activities, the ones that make you feel fabulous and happy. Now notice if you can take that feeling into all activities of the day. If you loose your fabulous feeling go back to imagining your favorite activity, regain the feeling, and carry it into your 'to dos' at hand. Notice if you can transform a dull job into something interesting by exchanging your old image of the job to the new one.

Perform all actions of this day with an increased positive energy. Recent studies have shown that the relationship between our brain's emotional centers and our muscular activation is indeed closer than previously assumed. And you know already that balanced muscular development is attractive.

Eighth Day

8

1. Repeat all the exercises from the previous day with the following modifications:

For the stand and sit exercise, remove your shoes and stand on rolled towels. Do the exercise 17 times with self-talk: "My muscles are supple and strong; my joints are well lubricated."

With an elastic band, rotate the torso 17 times with alternate arms pushing forward, while visualizing your ideal abdomen.

The focus for the day

Today you will focus on your **thymus gland**.

2. Place both hands palm down on the top center of your sternum. Imagine your thymus gland located below the sternum. Then vocalize a clear "Aaah…" and feel the sternum and thymus vibrating. Imagine your vocalization creating a sense of buoyancy in the thymus and opening and expanding your sternum, while relaxing the muscles of your shoulder and neck.

Repeat the thymus vocalization whenever you feel you need a rejuvenating break.

Ninth Day

1. Repeat all the exercises from the previous day with the following modifications:

For the stand and sit exercise, remove your shoes and stand on rolled towels. Do the exercise 18 times with self-talk: "My muscles are supple and strong; my joints are well lubricated."

Using an elastic band rotate the torso 18 times with alternate arms pushing forward, while visualizing your ideal abdomen.

The focus for the day

Today you will focus on your **nervous system**.

2. Stand upright and sense the nerves extending from the brainstem and spinal cord to the entire body. Lengthening like a host of delicate branches, they are able to reach the most distant corners of the body. Slowly drop forward by bending your back, one vertebra at a time, until you reach the floor. Bend the legs slightly and allow the head and arms to hang.

Imagine all your nerves loose and relaxed within their tissue sheaths, completely released like the boughs of a willow. Let the boughs and the

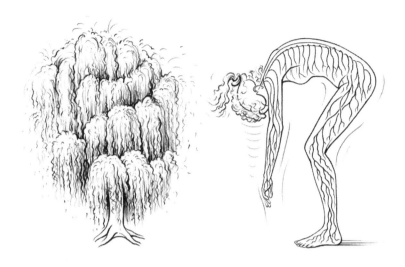

leaves sway gently to and fro. Then slowly straighten the spine, nerve-by-nerve, until you are upright. Sense the nerves embedded softly in supportive tissue.

Tenth Day

10

1. Repeat all the exercises from the previous day and modify as follows:

For the stand and sit exercise, stand on rolled towels. Do the exercise 20 times with self-talk: "My muscles are supple and strong; my joints are well lubricated."

Using an elastic band, rotate the torso 20 times with alternate arms pushing forward, while visualizing your ideal abdomen.

The focus for the day

Consider **what you have achieved** in 10 days.

2. As a final visualization for relaxation, imagine that within their protective sheaths, the nerves relax in a bed of down on a pile of featherbeds. They lie as calm and relaxed as babies within

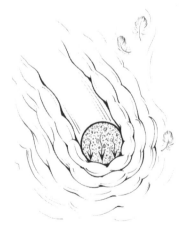

their protective sheaths. Sense all the nerve axons in the body lying comfortably, sighing as they enjoy such grand relaxation.

Naturally you can extend this daily program and enhance it with further exercises from the book. The long-term goal is, of course, to continue the program beyond 10 days, to maintain what you have achieved, avoid relapses, and continue to seek the balance between body and mind that radiates true beauty.

I encourage you.

Rate yourself on a scale of 1 to 10 (10 being the highest).

Day	overall feeling	face	posture	muscles	joints	organs	flexibility	ideal weight	mental attitude
1									
2									
3									
4									
5									
6									
7									
8									
9									
10									

Appendices

Resources for the Franklin Method® Related to this Book

Eric Franklin web page and contact information:

www.franklinmethod.com

Franklin balls, Franklin Mini Rollers, and bands (including Thera-Bands®) can be ordered from:

www.optp.com

For class and workshop schedule please consult our web page:

www.franklinmethod.com

Questions about classes and teacher training courses can be directed to:

info@franklin-methode.ch

For information on Franklin Method workshops, teacher training courses and products please contact:

info@franklin-methode.ch

About the Author

Eric Franklin has worked for more than twenty years as a successful dancer, choreographer, instructor, and author. From 1976 to 1979 he studied exercise science at the University of Zurich, from which he received a BS as an athletic instructor. During this time he was active in dance and ballet, furthering his knowledge at New York University's *Tisch School of the Arts*, from which he graduated in 1982 with a BFA.

Active as a choreographer since 1980, Eric Franklin has worked extensively in dance and theater in New York and Europe. He taught the *Schweizer Kunstturn-Nationalkader* for many years, instructed at the *Heilpaedagogischen Seminar Zuerich*, and has led numerous continuing education courses for physical therapists. Presently he is a guest teacher at the *Musikhochschule* in Dresden and Vienna, as well as at the *Royal Ballet* in London. He has also taught in the United States and Korea, and was invited to teach for China's first modern dance company.

Eric has been employing imaging techniques in his instruction since 1986. He is the founder and director of the *Institute for the Franklin Method®*. The Institute offers numerous courses, workshops, and training programs. (For further information, please see www.franklinmethod.com).

Eric Franklin's books published by Princeton Book Company, Publishers, are *Relax Your Neck—Liberate Your Shoulders, Pelvic Power*, and *Inner Focus, Outer Strength*.

For more information, go to www.dancehorizons.com

Other books include *Dynamic Alignment Through Imagery, Dance Imagery for Technique and Performance, Conditioning for Dance,* and *Ball and Imagery Exercises for Relaxed Shoulders and a Released Neck.*

Eric's books have been translated into German, Italian, Spanish, Czech, Chinese and Korean.

Index of Exercises